Series / Number 07-024

UNIDIMENSIONAL SCALING

JOHN P. McIVER
EDWARD G. CARMINES
Indiana University

SAGE PUBLICATIONS
The International Professional Publishers
Newbury Park   London   New Delhi

For information address:

 SAGE Publications, Inc.
2455 Teller Road
Newbury Park, California 91320
E-mail: order@sagepub.com

SAGE Publications Ltd.
6 Bonhill Street
London EC2A 4PU
United Kingdom

SAGE Publications India Pvt. Ltd.
M-32 Market
Greater Kailash I
New Delhi 110 048 India

Printed in the United States of America

International Standard Book Number 0-8039-1736-8

Library of Congress Catalog Card No. L.C. 81-52620

96 97 98 99 00 01 02 19 18 17 16 15 14 13

When citing a professional paper, please use the proper form. Remember to cite the correct Sage University Paper series title and include the paper number. One of the two following formats can be adapted (depending on the style manual used):

(1) IVERSEN, GUDMUND R. and NORPOTH, HELMUT (1976) *Analysis of Variance*. Sage University Paper Series on Quantitative Applications in the Social Sciences, 07-001. Newbury Park, CA: Sage.

or

(2) Iversen, G. R., & Norpoth, H. (1976). *Analysis of variance* (Sage University Paper Series on Quantitative Applications in the Social Sciences, series no. 07-001). Newbury Park, CA: Sage.

CONTENTS

Editor's Introduction

In UNIDIMENSIONAL SCALING, John McIver and Ted Carmines provide an introductory treatment of Thurstone scaling, Likert scaling, Guttman scaling, and unfolding theory. We are most pleased to add this to the list of topics covered by the QUANTITATIVE APPLICATIONS IN THE SOCIAL SCIENCES series, as it is among the two or three topics that have been most often requested by pedagogues around the nation. There has been a dearth of good introductory treatments of these topics during recent years, and yet the demand holds strong, both for undergraduate courses and introductory graduate seminars in measurement and scaling. It is our hope that this paper fills the need, and we believe it has.

After discussing the nature of measurement and scaling, and such topics as multidimensional versus unidimensional scaling, McIver and Carmines focus the bulk of their attention on Likert scaling and Guttman scaling, devoting two chapters to the latter. After explaining the basic elements of these scaling techniques and their application, they address several of the more important problems and issues in Guttman scaling, such as how to deal with missing data, how to analyze polytomous rather than dichotomous items, significance tests, and so on. Their advice throughout is practical, and novices should be in a position to read this monograph and then proceed directly to the application of these scaling techniques in their research projects. The techniques are simple ones, designed to solve simple problems with relatively simple models, and as such the material can be presented clearly and without obfuscation in a short monograph. We believe McIver and Carmines have succeeded in doing so. Finally, the monograph ends with a presentation and discussion of Coombs's unfolding theory in a single dimension. This is a useful introduction to unfolding models, and is a good starting point for the uninitiated.

Throughout the presentation, McIver and Carmines make ample use of substantive examples, including (1) an extended example of the measurement of self-esteem as an illustration of Likert scaling; (2) lengthy examples of voting in the U.S. Senate on the creation of a Consumer Protection Agency and of the structure of participation in American politics as illustrations of Guttman scaling; and (3) examples of the measurement of cosmopolitanism and trust in government to illustrate the potential uses of unfolding theory in social science research. They argue that unfolding theory has not received the attention it deserves and that social scientists ought to consider its applications more seriously than they have to date.

UNIDIMENSIONAL SCALING serves as an excellent introduction to scaling generally, and should serve nicely as a lead-in to MULTIDIMEN-SIONAL SCALING by Joseph Kruskal and Myron Wish, published earlier in this series. It is also a useful supplement to Carmines's earlier effort in this series, RELIABILITY AND VALIDITY ASSESSMENT, with Richard Zeller. Unidimensional scaling techniques are used broadly in the social sciences, particularly but not exclusively in those disciplines that study attitudes, preferences, and perceptions, including: psychologists, most particularly social psychologists, who have pioneered the study of attitudes and scaling analysis; sociologists, particularly those who specialize in social psychology and political sociology; marketing researchers and journalists; political scientists, particularly those specializing in political behavior and public opinion; educational psychologists; and many others. For students in these and other fields, this paper should serve as an excellent introduction to scaling analysis, and it will no doubt stimulate the student's interest and desire to conduct relevant research in each of these diverse fields of inquiry.

—John L. Sullivan, Series Editor

UNIDIMENSIONAL SCALING

JOHN P. McIVER
EDWARD G. CARMINES
Indiana University

1. INTRODUCTION

Among the many changes that have occurred in American politics since the mid-1960s, none is perhaps as potentially significant as the sharp decline in citizens' trust in government (Miller, 1974a, 1974b; Jennings and Niemi, 1981). While the precise meaning and implications of this decline are a source of considerable controversy (Citrin, 1974; Miller, 1974; Abramson and Finifter, 1981), at least on the surface it seems to reflect a profound loss of confidence in the government's performance. Civil rights, Vietnam, Watergate—these "events" are no doubt linked to this decline in political trust. A fundamental question is whether the trend is merely temporary, being a reaction to the heightened political tensions of the 1960s and 1970s, or signifies a basic and permanent withdrawal of support for the political system.

The point we want to emphasize is that neither this question nor most other important questions about this political phenomenon can be answered unless the theoretical construct of political trust can be measured in a useful and meaningful way. In other words, it is necessary to obtain a valid and reliable indicator of political trust if its distribution, causes, and consequences are to be investigated and understood. In the broadest terms, this empirical indicator may be referred to as a *scale*. In this particular instance, the scale is composed of a set of attitudinal items intended to capture empirically the essential meaning of political trust. The following five items make up an often-used political trust scale:

(1) Do you think that people in the government waste a lot of the money we pay in taxes, waste some of it, or don't waste very much of it?

AUTHORS' NOTE: *We would like to thank Patty Smith, Teresa Therrien, and Marsha Porter of the Workshop in Political Theory and Policy Analysis at Indiana University for*

(2) How much of the time do you think you can trust the government in Washington to do what is right—just about always, most of the time, or only some of the time?

(3) Would you say the government is pretty much run by a few big interests looking out for themselves or that it is run for the benefit of all the people?

(4) Do you think that almost all of the people running the government are smart people, or do you think that quite a few of them don't seem to know what they are doing?

(5) Do you think that quite a few of the people running the government are crooked, not very many are, or do you think hardly any of them are crooked?

There are a number of different ways of combining these items into a scale depending on the purpose(s) the resulting scale is to serve. Each of these different purposes is associated with a specific scaling model, which may be defined as an "internally consistent plan for the development of a new measure" (Nunnally, 1978: 35). The purpose of this monograph is to provide an introduction to scaling theory and to discuss several unidimensional scaling models. Specifically, we focus on Thurstone scaling, Likert scaling, Guttman scaling, and unfolding theory. The purpose of this chapter is to present an overview of some basic considerations in scaling, laying the foundation for our treatment of these scaling models.

Purposes of Scaling

Scaling models may be employed for three related but distinct purposes (Coombs, 1964; Weisberg, 1974).[1] First, scaling analysis may perform a hypothesis-testing purpose. Political scientists, for example, may test the hypothesis that there is a single dimension, ideology (e.g., liberalism), that underlies voters' preferences for different political candidates. In this case, the scaling model is used as a criterion to evaluate the relative fit of a given set of observed data to a specific model. Second, scaling may be employed for the purpose of simply describing a data structure, that is, for discovering the latent dimensions underlying a set of obtained observations. This would be the case, for example, if psychologists attempted to specify the dimensions underlying the perceived loudness of various sounds. No hypothesis is necessarily being tested here. Instead, the purpose of the analysis is mainly exploratory. Whether the primary purpose of

their assistance in preparing this monograph. Gail Bumgarner, Richard G. Niemi, Leroy Rieselbach, and John L. Sullivan provided useful comments on an earlier version of the manuscript.

the analysis is confirmatory (the testing of a specific hypothesis) or exploratory, the technique can be used to derive and construct a scale, in which case it is a scaling method. In this third instance the purpose of scaling is to develop a unidimensional scale on which individuals can be given scores. Their scores on the particular scale can then be related to other measures of interest. Sociologists, for example, may construct a scale for measuring socioeconomic status that can be correlated with a variety of attitudinal and behavioral measures. While all scaling models can be used in these three capacities, a particular model may lend itself to one type of usage more than another. In other words, scaling models differ in the extent to which they have been employed for these various purposes.

Approaches to Scaling

Scaling models may be used to scale persons, stimuli, or both persons and stimuli.[2] Likert scaling is an example of a scaling model employed only to scale subjects. In Likert scaling, individuals are presented with a list of statements about a single topic (e.g., the President) and are instructed to respond to each statement in terms of their degree of agreement or disagreement. Thus, this scaling model involves a single type of stimuli and a single type of response. The remaining problem, then, is to combine responses for each individual in such a way that valid and reliable differences among individuals can be represented. Likert scaling is considered a subject-centered or person-centered approach to scaling since only subjects (or persons) receive scale scores (see Torgerson, 1958).

Instead of scaling persons, however, researchers are sometimes interested in scaling stimuli. Consider, for example, a group of people who are asked to judge the weight of a given set of objects. In this instance the objects are quantified with respect to a particular attribute—their perceived weight. It is the stimuli rather than the persons that are scaled in this example.[3] The same would be true if the group was asked to rate the loudness of tones, the sweetness of candy, or pleasantness of interviewees. In each of these examples the task set for the subject is to evaluate the stimuli with respect to some designated attribute.

What if the researcher wanted to scale both subjects and stimuli? This involves a third approach to scaling which is referred to as the response approach. As Torgerson (1958: 48) observes, "the task set for the subject is to respond to a stimulus on the basis of the position of the stimulus in relation to the subject's own position with respect to the attribute." The subject, for example, might be asked to pick a particular candidate from a list that is closest to his ideal candidate or pick a particular statement from a set of statements with which he is in closest agreement. In either case, the response would reflect jointly his own position on the attribute in question as well as how the stimuli related to the attribute. Thus, the subject's own attitude plays an important role in his response. As we shall discuss in a later chapter, Guttman scaling is an example of the response approach in which both subjects and stimuli can be assigned scale values.

In summary, scaling models can be distinguished according to whether they are intended to scale persons, stimuli, or both persons and stimuli. This is one of the fundamental distinctions among scaling models.

Item Trace Lines of Scaling Models

Many scaling models can be distinguished by their trace lines. A trace line is simply a curve describing the relationship between the probability of a specific response to an item (e.g., the probability of agreeing to a statement about whether you feel as if you are being watched) and the attribute that the item is supposed to measure (paranoia). Each of the scaling models discussed in this monograph is associated with a particular type of trace line. Indeed, this is the basic theoretical difference among scaling models. Remember, however, as you read through the next five chapters, that while item trace lines are supposed to take on a certain shape for each scaling model, they may not do so. Trace lines are not observed, but rather they are theoretical concepts. Empirical items may have trace lines that are inappropriate for the scales in which they are included. Indeed, this is frequently a criticism of existing scales.

Trace lines permit us to make an initial distinction between scaling models as deterministic or probabilistic. Deterministic models do not provide for measurement error. Consequently, the probability of a given response to an item can only be zero or one at any point on the underlying continuum of the attribute being measured. Probabilistic models, on the other hand, do permit random measurement errors. Thus the probability of a response to an item may vary from zero to one and is not restricted to these extreme positions.

Figure 1 provides three examples of the trace lines of dichotomous items: The first is typical of items appropriate for Thurstone scales; the second is the trace line of an item suitable for Likert scales; items used in Guttman scales have trace lines similar to the third curve.

The first two trace lines are associated with probabilistic scaling models. Guttman scaling is a deterministic model as the final trace line in Figure 1 illustrates. As we turn to each scaling model, the importance of the item trace lines for scale interpretation will become more obvious.

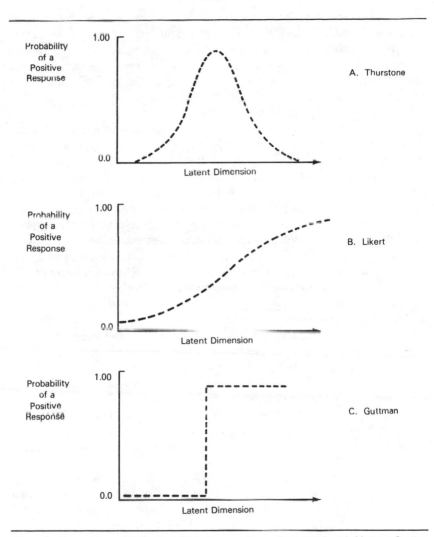

Figure 1: Trace Lines for Typical Dichotomous Items Associated with Various Scaling Models

Types of Data

A third important difference among scaling models relates to the type of data that is appropriate to the model. Coombs (1964) has indicated that there are four basic kinds of data. *Preferential choice data* involve the ranking of objects (i.e., stimuli) according to some criterion or purpose. For example, voters might be asked to rank a set of presidential candidates according to the voter's preferred choice from most preferred to least preferred. Another example would be if a group of individuals was asked to rank cities according to how desirable it would be to live in them. It is clear that preferential choice data represent a response approach to scaling since the ranking of objects according to the subject's preference necessarily involves both the subject's own position on the attribute and how the stimuli are perceived to relate to the attribute.

A second type of data described by Coombs is *single-stimulus data.* As the name implies, single-stimulus data involve the subject responding to stimuli one at a time. There is no explicit ranking or comparison of stimuli. Thus, in contrast to the illustrations above, one would be asked whether he approved of a particular candidate or would choose to live in a particular city. Notice that single-stimulus data, depending on their essential purpose, could be used to scale stimuli, subjects, or both stimuli and subjects. For example, Likert scaling is based on single-stimulus data and, as we have said, leads to the scaling of individuals. On the other hand, if individuals were asked to estimate the weight of given objects one at a time, then one could consider this process leading to the scaling of the stimuli themselves.

A third type of data involves *stimulus comparison data.* In this situation the individual is presented with a set of stimuli and asked to select the one that has more or less of the specific attribute in question than the others. To give a practical example, two candidates, two cigars, and two bourbons are presented to individuals and they are asked to select the more honest politician, the milder cigar, and the more mellow bourbon, respectively. In this instance the individual's own position or preference is not directly engaged; instead, the evaluation is assumed to reflect differences among the stimuli, not the individuals. Thus, stimulus comparison data represent a stimulus-oriented approach to scaling.

The fourth type of data discussed by Coombs is called *similarities data.* All pairs of stimuli are formed, and "the individuals will be presented with these pairs and asked in which pair the members are more alike" (Coombs, 1964: 14). For example, a group of presidential candidates might be put into all of the pairs possible given the number of candidates. These pairs could then be presented two at a time to individuals who are asked which of the dyads contains the more similar candidates. In contrast to the other types of data, no instructions are given to individuals about the dimensions on which the dyads are to be compared. On the contrary, this is precisely what the researcher hopes to discover in his investigation. It is important to realize that similarities data also involve the scaling of stimuli, not individuals. In this respect it is similar to stimulus comparison data.

Multidimensional Versus Unidimensional Models

A fourth characteristic on which scaling models can be distinguished is whether the models are multidimensional or unidimensional in nature. As we shall discuss later, the concept of dimensionality is complex, primarily because the substantive and technical meaning of the term is specific to the particular scaling model. That is, dimensionality means different things for different scaling models. For the present purposes, however, it is sufficient to understand at an intuitive level the distinction between unidimensionality and multidimensionality.

As the name implies, "unidimensional scaling theory and techniques are aimed at selecting a set of data items that can be empirically demonstrated to correspond to a single social-psychological dimension" (Gordon, 1977: 28). That is, unidimensional scaling is relevant to those situations in which it is presumed that there exists a single, fundamental dimension underlying a set of observations (i.e., data items). If a psychologist, for example, is attempting to devise or evaluate a scale intended to measure a single personality trait, then unidimensional scaling models and techniques would be appropriate for this purpose. Similarly, unidimensional scaling models would be relevant to a situation in which people were asked to evaluate the qualifications of different presidential candidates. The presumption would be that there is a single common dimension on which candidates are arrayed. Thus, unidimensional models can be used to scale persons, stimuli, or both persons and stimuli. They can also be used in conjunction with each of the types of data described above. That is, one can evaluate the degree to which a single dimension underlies preferential choice data, single-stimulus data, stimulus comparison data, or similarities data.

In contrast to unidimensional models, multidimensional scaling models explicitly allow for the possibility—indeed, the great likelihood—that there is more than a single dimension that underlies a set of observations. The scaling of subjects or stimuli (or both subjects and stimuli) is no longer viewed in a unidimensional space. Rather, multidimensional scaling concerns the location of any object in multidimensional space. As Gordon (1977: 26) has stated, "instead of simply measuring the amount of a particular property of an object, the problem is simultaneously to classify the object according to two or more properties."

Multidimensional scaling techniques can be used to determine the existence of a single latent dimension (as defined within that particular scaling model) underlying a set of obtained observations. The reverse, however, is not true. If a set of observations is not scalable according to a particular unidimensional scaling model, then a multidimensional model may be more appropriate for the data. On the other hand, this evidence may be an indication that the data are simply unscalable—for multidimensional models as well as unidimensional models.

Given the greater power and flexibility of multidimensional models, the question naturally arises as to why there continues to be substantial interest in unidimensional scaling models.

First, unidimensional scaling techniques are easier to understand and apply than multidimensional methods. Second, there are some conditions under which unidimensional scaling is a necessary prior step to multidimensional scaling (for further discussion of this point see Gordon, 1977: 25-30). Moreover, on a purely intellectual basis, exposure to and experience working with unidimensional methods is quite useful for understanding multidimensional scaling techniques. Indeed it is no exaggeration to say that a relatively thorough knowledge of the nature of unidimensional scaling models is necessary for even a rudimentary understanding of more complex multidimensional models. The logical order of their relationship to one another is analogous to that of the relationship between univariate and multivariate statistics. In each case, the latter presupposes comprehension of the former.

The final and most important reason why unidimensional scaling models continue to be of substantial interest is that they are isomorphic with the primary type of concepts devised by social scientists. Shively (1980), for example, has argued that social scientists should strive to develop and use unidimensional concepts because they are more susceptible to theory-relevant research (also see Clausen and Van Horn, 1977). Multidimensional concepts, on the other hand, typically hamper such research because they are too ambiguous in terms of their meaning, too difficult to measure in a clear and precise manner, and too theoretically oriented themselves. Their complexity and ambiguity renders them less optimal for the development and assessment of social science theories.

In other words, using unidimensional scaling models to measure unidimensional concepts puts the theory construction and the measurement strategy on the same analytical level. It is for this reason that there exists literally hundreds of unidimensional scales designed to measure individual differences on all kinds of psychological, sociological, and political dimensions (Robinson et al., 1968, 1969, 1973). These scales allow the social scientist to array individuals in terms of the relative magnitude that they possess of the property in question—to score individuals in terms of a particular attribute.

The foregoing discussion suggests that unidimensional models are especially useful for scaling persons or subjects. Indeed, if various individual properties can be scaled according to unidimensional criteria, then the researcher has fulfilled an explicit theoretical purpose. He has developed a scale that is isomorphic with the theoretical language developed in the social sciences. As we have indicated above, this is a major goal of the social sciences.

Multiitem Versus Single-Item Scales

While unidimensional scales are quite useful for the measurement of a variety of individual properties, these scales should be made up of multiple items rather than a single item. There are several reasons why multiitem scales are superior to single-item scales (Nunnally, 1978: 66-68). First, it is very unlikely that a single item can fully represent a complex theoretical concept or any specific attribute for that matter. For example, no single item in a clinical rating evaluation will allow a psychologist to measure accurately and validly a person's level of anxiety. Second, single-item measures lack precision because they cannot discriminate among fine degrees of an attribute. In fact, commonly used dichotomous items can only distinguish between two levels of the attribute. Third, single-item measures are usually less reliable than multiitem scales (for a demonstration, see Zeller and Carmines, 1980). That is, they are more prone to random error. Chance or random error is involved in any type of measurement. However, as Nunnally (1978: 67) observes, "this unreliability averages out when scores on numerous items are summed to obtain a total score, which then frequently is highly reliable."

The most fundamental problem with single-item measures is not merely that they tend to be less valid, less accurate, and less reliable than their multiitem equivalents. It is, rather, that because they provide only a single measurement, the social scientist rarely has sufficient information to estimate their measurement properties. Thus, their degree of validity, accuracy, and reliability is often unknowable. The absence of this vital information can sometimes lead us to overlook the serious deficiencies of single-item measures. But as Blalock (1970: 111) has observed, "with a single measure of each variable, one can remain blissfully unaware of the possibility of measurement [error], but in no sense will this make his inferences more valid."

Conclusion

This chapter has presented a brief overview of scaling. While numerous distinctions can be made among scaling models, we have concentrated on five that are particularly relevant for the purpose of this monograph. The first distinction has to do with whether the scaling model is intended to scale persons, stimuli, or both persons and stimuli. Second, scaling models are distinguished by the trace lines. Most generally, trace lines identify models as deterministic or probabilistic. Third, it is also necessary to understand the type of data that is appropriate to a particular scaling model. Following Coombs (1964), we have identified four basic types of data: preferential choice data, single-stimulus data, stimulus comparison data, and similarities data.

A fourth basic distinction among scaling models is whether they are unidimensional or multidimensional in nature. While the latter are certainly more complex than the former, they are not necessarily more appropriate in all research situations. On the contrary, we have suggested that for both practical and theoretical reasons, unidimensional scaling models will continue to play a major role in the social sciences.

Finally, we have pointed out the severe limitations of single-item measures. Whenever possible social scientists should employ multiple-item measures of theoretical concepts. An important distinction among scaling models is the criteria used for choosing items to be included in the scale. These criteria are not the same for different scaling models, but differ depending on the purposes and assumptions of the scaling analysis.

This chapter has outlined some basic considerations in scaling, especially in regard to the social sciences. The remaining chapters in this monograph expand upon this discussion, focusing exclusively on unidimensional scaling models. Chapter 2 treats Thurstone scaling briefly; Chapter 3 provides a detailed exposition of Likert scaling. Chapter 4 provides an introduction to Guttman scaling while Chapter 5 examines some special issues that arise with regard to this scaling model. Chapter 6 treats unfolding theory in the unidimensional case. Finally, Chapter 7 compares these last three scaling models, focusing primarily on their different conceptions of dimensionality.

2. THURSTONE SCALING

We begin our consideration of scaling models by examining briefly the contributions of Louis Thurstone, a psychologist at the University of Chicago. Not only was Thurstone one of the first psychologists to propose systematic procedures for measuring attitudes but also his research led to the development of three related but distinct methods of scaling: paired comparisons, successive intervals, and equal-appearing intervals (Thurstone, 1927, 1929; Thurstone and Chave, 1929). First, we outline the common theoretical justification for Thurstone scaling, the Law of

Comparative Judgment, and then discuss the most popular of these scaling models, the method of equal-appearing intervals.

The Law of Comparative Judgment

Thurstone was mainly concerned with the fundamental problem of how psychological stimuli could be measured and compared with one another. The measurement of physical objects, in contrast, is simple and straightforward. If a scientist wanted to discover the weight of each of a set of objects, for example, he simply placed each object on a scale and recorded its measured weight. The resulting objects could then be ordered from the lightest to the heaviest. If no scale was available, however, the process of ordering the objects by their relative weight becomes considerably more problematic because it unavoidably involves individual judgments. We could, for example, ask each of a group of individuals to arrange the objects from lightest to heaviest by having each individual lift each of the objects one at a time. Alternatively, we could present the objects in all possible pairs and ask each person which member of the dyad was the heavier. In either case, we could obtain an ordering of the weight of the objects based on the comparative judgments of the group of individuals.

Thurstone recognized that this was precisely the situation of the social scientist attempting to measure psychological (nonphysical) stimuli—measuring the weight of objects without the use of a scale. And the solution must also lie in the use of human judgments. To take a practical example, consider the situation in which a group of individuals is given a list of occupations and asked to evaluate each according to its relative prestige. The list of occupations represents the stimuli, and the presumption is that each can be ordered along a psychological continuum with respect to the degree of prestige each possesses. The law of comparative judgments presumes that for each stimulus—in this case, each occupation—there exists a most frequently occuring response, which is referred to as its *modal discriminal process* on the psychological continuum. Stated most simply, each individual makes a discrimination or response involving a judgment as to the relative degree of prestige of each occupation. It is not assumed that each stimulus always evokes the same discriminal process for different individuals or even for the same individual at different times. Thus, while the occupation of medical doctor will elicit a modal response from the group of individuals as regards its prestige, this modal discriminal process will not characterize all of the responses. It is typically assumed that the distribution of all discriminal processes aroused by any given stimulus is normal about the modal discriminal process. The normal distribution can be described by two parameters—its mean and standard deviation. Moreover, the mean, median, and mode have the same value for any normal distribution. The mean discriminal process is taken as the scale value for the particular stimulus, and it standard deviation is designated as the *discriminal dispersion* for the stimulus. Any two occupations may thus differ in terms of their modal discriminal processes, that is, their scale values and their discriminal dispersions. Now the list of occupations can be ordered along the psychological continuum representing prestige by calculating their scale values and arranging them from most to least prestigious.

The basic assumption underlying the law of comparative judgment is that the degree to which any two stimuli can be discriminated is a direct function of the difference in their status as regards the attribute in question.[4] To continue with our example, presumably most respondents would judge the medical doctor to be higher in prestige than the automobile mechanic. Their relative scale scores would reflect this difference. If two stimuli are judged to have exactly the same scale score— that is, one half of the respondents considering occupation A to be more prestigious than occupation B and the other half judging B to be more prestigious than A—then they are considered to have the same amount of the property. Thus, the placement of occupations on the prestige continuum should reflect the degree to which respondents can discriminate among the perceived prestige of the various occupations. The greater the distance between any two occupations on the continuum, the greater the extent to which the respondents have agreed that one of the occupations is more prestigious than the other occupation. Conversely, the smaller the distance between any two occupations on the continuum, the more confusion exists about the relative prestige of the two occupations. The degree to which any two occupations can be discriminated is a direct reflection of their perceived differences in prestige.

Each of the three scaling methods developed by Thurstone—the method of paired comparisons, the method of successive intervals, and the method of equal-appearing intervals—may be considered a different operationalization of the basic Law of Comparative Judgment.[5]

Method of Equal-Appearing Intervals

Thurstone was concerned mainly with two fundamental aspects of scale construction: the selection of statements that make up the scale and the procedures by which scale values could be assigned to the items. He presumed that in developing a particular attitude scale it would be necessary to obtain a large set of statements (approximately 100) that would reflect all shades of opinion toward the object or phenomenon. It would thus be necessary to consult many different types of sources of information, including newspapers, magazines, as well as a variety of other documents to represent various degrees of positive and negative sentiment. Thurstone also pointed out that the items should be clear, precise, and express a single opinion. Over the years a number of researchers have noted the desirable characteristics of attitude items. The following abbreviated list has been compiled by Edwards (1957: 13, 14; also see the discussion by Robinson et al., 1968: 9-21):

(1) Avoid statements that refer to the past rather than to the present.
(2) Avoid statements that are factual or capable of being interpreted as factual.
(3) Avoid statements that may be interpreted in more than one way.
(4) Avoid statements that are irrelevant to the psychological object under consideration.
(5) Avoid statements that are likely to be endorsed by almost everyone or by almost no one.
(6) Select statements that are believed to cover the entire range of the affective scale of interest.
(7) Keep the language of the statements simple, clear, and direct.
(8) Each statement should contain only one complete thought.
(9) Statements containing universals such as all, always, none, and never often introduce ambiguity and should be avoided.
(10) Words such as only, just, merely, and others of a similar nature should be used with care and moderation in writing statements.
(11) Whenever possible, statements should be in the form of simple sentences rather than in the form of compound or complex sentences.

After the items have been initially chosen to reflect accurately and completely the particular attitude, they are submitted to a group of persons acting as judges. Each judge is instructed to evaluate the statements in terms of the degree of favorableness/unfavorableness they indicate toward the object or phenomenon being investigated. In the method of equal-appearing intervals, the judges are asked to sort the items into 11 piles, with the first pile (A) representing the most favorable or positive feelings toward the object, the middle pile (F) indicating neutral sentiments, and the final pile (K) representing the most unfavorable or negative feelings. In essence, the judges are giving each of the approximately 100 statements a scale value from 1 (most favorable) to 11 (most unfavorable).

Two pieces of information are then usually used to select a much smaller number of items for the final scale. The *median* for each of the items is used as its scale value. Obviously, the lower the median, the more favorable the judges consider the statement to be as an attitude toward the object under investigation; the higher the median, the more unfavorable the expressed intent of the item. As an example, consider the following three items taken from Thurstone and Chave's (1929: 51-63, 78) attitude toward the Church scale:

(1) I believe the church is the greatest institution in America today (scale value: .2).
(2) I believe in religion, but I seldom go to church (scale value: 5.4).
(3) I think the church is a hindrance to religion for it still depends on magic, superstition, and myth (scale value: 9.6).

In addition to the median, the *interquartile range* is computed for each item. This statistic is a measure of the spread of the middle 50% of the judgments. When there is high agreement among the judges concerning the location of the item on the scale, the interquartile range will be a small value. Conversely, a large interquartile range indicates that there is substantial disagreement among the judges as to the degree of the attribute possessed by a statement.

The following criteria are applied for the selection of the final items to be included in the attitudinal scale. First, the items are chosen with median values distributed along the full range of the scale. This criterion ensures that the set of items spans the entire attitudinal continuum. Second, given a set of statements with the same or very similar median values, those with the *smallest* interquartile ranges are selected because they reflect less disagreement among the judges concerning the content of the item. Since disagreement is taken as a sign of item ambiguity, this criterion is intended to reduce the pool of items to those that are least ambivalent in representing a specific shade of attitude. Finally, in the equal-appearing interval method of scaling, the items are chosen to fall at as many equal-appearing intervals along the scale as possible.

Since many of the original items will have been eliminated because they are inconsistent with one or more of these criteria, the remaining items forming the scale (approximately 20 to 22 items) should cover the entire attitudinal continuum, be relatively evenly spaced across the full continuum, and have relatively small interquartile values. The statements are then arranged in either random order or according to their scale values and presented to subjects with instructions to check those with which they accept or agree. The average scale value of those items chosen represents the person's attitude toward the object in question.

Limitations of Thurstone Scaling

While Thurstone scaling represented a major contribution to the systematic measurement of attitudes, the approach proved to be problematic in a number of regards. First, the method assumes that the items have determinate scale positions that are the same for subjects as judges (Scott, 1968: 229). However, judges are asked to respond to the items not in terms of their own attitudes toward the phenomenon (as are subjects), but in terms of the placement of the items on the continuum. As Scott (1968: 229) observes, "the model requires that differences in judged location of a particular item are 'random' and do not depend on systematic characteristics of the judges." Yet, it has been found that judges with extremist attitudes toward the phenomenon, either positive or negative, do not discriminate effectively among moderate items (Scott, 1968). More generally, it is often unrealistic to presume that the judge's own attitude is independent of his item judgments, as required by the model.

Second, since the tasks for the judges and subjects are different, there is a substantial possibility that the intended dimension may not determine the subjects' responses to the items. In other words, subjects may well respond to the items for reasons that were unanticipated in the construction of the scale, resulting in an invalid measuring instrument.

A related limitation of Thurstone scaling is that it presumes but provides no direct evidence of the unidimensionality of the scale. Thurstone focused on the assignment of the items along the dimension, but took for granted that persons' responses could be adequately represented on the same dimension.

Finally, the construction of Thurstone scales requires an inordinate amount of labor because of both the use of judges and the need to assign scale values to each of the original items. Thus, as a pragmatic matter, it is often easier and simpler to construct equally valid and reliable scales based on other models.[6]

Conclusion

Thurstone scaling represented a major advancement in the scaling of psychological stimuli. Building on his Law of Comparative Judgment, Thurstone introduced three methods of scaling: paired comparisons, successive intervals, and equal-appearing intervals. The underlying logic and basic procedures involved in constructing a scale based on the method of equal-appearing intervals have been discussed in this chapter. While

Thurstone scaling techniques were quite popular during the 1920s and 1930s, they are not employed widely today because of a number of limitations discusssed earlier.

Both Likert and Guttman scaling methods overcome these limitations of Thurstone scaling. Likert was especially interested in simplifying the procedures for constructing attitude scales and in using intensity-scaled responses for each item. Guttman, in turn, focused directly on the fundamental problem of assessing the degree of unidimensionality found among a set of scale items. We shall examine Likert's method of scaling in Chapter 3 while Chapters 4 and 5 will be concerned with Guttman scaling.

3. LIKERT SCALING

Introduction

No scaling model has more intuitive appeal than the Likert scale. Very generally, any scale obtained by adding together the response scores of its constituent items is referred to as a Likert or "summative" scale. Alternatively, the term *linear composite* is used to designate such a scale. We often find these scales in our everyday lives. The winner of a baseball game is the team with the highest summated rating, that is, the team with the highest total of runs as computed by summing the runs scored in each of the team's nine "tests" or innings at bat. IQ scores, the sum of the correct answers on an "intelligence" test, affect our lives both in school and out. Even our job status may be related to summated ratings—both aptitude tests prior to hiring and performance ratings (possibly prior to firing) are often based on the simple action of summing a series of related criteria to arrive at a final evaluation of the employee.

Summative rating scales are also found throughout the social sciences (Robinson et al., 1968, 1969, 1973). Many of these scales were created in accordance with Likert's procedures for selecting a set of items that measure the same attitude. For example, each of the scales designed to measure various aspects of an "authoritarian personality" (Adorno et al., 1950)—the F (Fascism) scale, the E (Ethnocentrism) scale, and the AS (Anti-Semitism) scale—was empirically identified and refined using Likert procedures.

In briefest outline, Likert scaling may be described in the following manner. A set of items, composed of approximately an equal number of favorable and unfavorable statements concerning the attitude object, is given to a group of subjects. They are asked to respond to each statement in terms of their own degree of agreement or disagreement. Typically, they are instructed to select one of five responses: strongly agree, agree, undecided, disagree, or strongly disagree. The specific responses to the items are combined so that individuals with the most favorable attitudes will have the highest scores while individuals with the least favorable (or most unfavorable) attitudes will have the lowest scores.

While not all summative scales are created according to Likert's specific procedures, all such scales share the basic logic associated with Likert scaling. It is to this underlying logic that we now turn.

Constructing a Likert Scale

The Likert approach to scaling consists of three interrelated tasks: (1) item construction, (2) item scoring, and (3) item selection. Underlying these tasks is a series of assumptions about the nature of the stimuli and the final attitude of scale.[7]

As we noted in Chapter 1, Likert's procedure is "subject-centered" (Torgerson, 1958), that is, its purpose is to scale respondents, not attitude items. This is in contrast to the purpose of Guttman scaling in which both resondents and questionnaire items are scaled relative to the attitude in question. In Likert scaling all *systematic* variation in the responses to the stimuli is attributed to differences among the respondents. The stimuli are considered replications of one another.

This model permits very lenient assumptions about the individual components of an attitude scale. Indeed, Nunnally (1978) suggests that because each item may contain considerable measurement error and/or specificity, the importance of this additive model is that it does not take any particular item very seriously. We assume that each item is monotonically related to the underlying attitude continuum (see Figure 1). In other words, the more favorable (unfavorable) a respondent's attitude, the higher (lower) his or her expected score for the item would be. Note that this assumption does not imply that each item has exactly the same relationship with the latent attitude; rather, each item may have a unique monotonic trace line.

Two additional assumptions are implied by the process of combining individual items into a summative scale. First, the sum of the item trace lines is expected to be monotonic (and approximately linear) with respect to the attitude measured. Second, we assume that the items as a group measure only the attribute under investigation. In other words, all items to be linearly combined should only be related to a single common factor. The sum of these items is expected to contain all the important information contained in the individual items.

These assumptions are not strict. For some purposes and under some linear models, we can add additional constraints. Under various test theory models, for instance, we may insist on linear trace lines and specific population distributions of responses. Other trace line models with specific types of monotonic trace lines include Lazarsfeld's (1954) latent distance model and the normal ogive model. These considerations, however, are not crucial to the Likert approach.

Having designed an initial set of items to measure a particular attribute, the next phase of scaling requires evaluation of this item set. Are these items related to one another and by inference to the construct they are supposed to measure? Which items may be combined to form the best single measure? Which items apparently fail at their given task and should be dropped from the final set of items which will comprise the scale? In this section we discuss several of the criteria suggested by Likert for dealing with these questions.

Likert originally proposed two types of "item analysis" methods to evaluate the ability of the individual items to measure the attribute measured by the total scale: correlation analysis and analysis based on the "criterion of internal consistency."

Computing correlations between each item and the sum (or average) of all items is the first "objective check" suggested by Likert:

> If a zero or very low correlation coefficient is obtained, it indicates that the statement fails to measure that which the rest of the statements measure. Such statements will be called undifferentiating [Murphy and Likert, 1938: 285].

It makes little sense to combine unrelated items into a total sum since undifferentiating items contribute little useful information to the total. Indeed, they may actually decrease the reliability and/or validity of the scale. Consequently, such items should not be retained in the final measuring instrument.

Because Likert scaling was developed prior to the advent of high-speed computers, the calculation of correlation coefficients was quite laborious, especially with large data sets. Likert, therefore, devised a second type of item analysis known as the criterion of internal consistency:

> In using the criterion of internal consistency, the reactions of the group that constitute one extreme in the particular attitude being measured are compared with the reactions of the group that constitute the other extreme. . . . If, a statement is undifferentiating it will not discriminate the two groups, i.e., the high group will not score

appreciably higher than the low group upon that statement [Murphy and Likert, 1938: 289-290].

The logic of this criterion is also not difficult to understand. An item that elicits an identical response from groups that presumably have sharply different views is obviously a poor indicator of the attitude in question. On the other hand, an item that clearly discriminates between the two extreme groups is exactly what is required in the scale. Initially the criterion was interpreted as a simple comparison of the difference between mean responses to an individual item of high and low subgroups on the initial scale. These subgroups are often operationalized as the 25% of respondents at each extreme of the scale. The size of these subgroups is not restricted, however, and may be greater or less than 25%.

The criterion of internal consistency was later modified to account for differences in subgroup size as well as different distributions of responses between subgroups. The critical ratio or t test evaluates subgroup mean differences *relative to item score variances* (Green, 1954; Edwards, 1957).

The critical ratio is:

$$t = (X_H - X_L) / \sqrt{(S_H^2/n_H) + (S_L^2/n_L)} \qquad [1]$$

where X_i is the mean item response of subgroup i, S_i^2 is the item variance of subgroup i, and n_i is the size of subgroup i. The critical ratio provides a more accurate indication of the degree to which an item differentiates between high and low subgroups by incorporating the distribution of responses by subgroup into the evaluation of mean differences. If two items are identically discriminating in terms of the subgroup mean differences, but the subgroups are very homogeneous in their responses to the first item and much less so with respect to the second item, the critical ratio is sensitive to the greater differentiating power of the first item.

Which type of item analysis should one choose? Likert's concern about the labor costs of computing correlation coefficients has little validity now. Furthermore, Green (1954) points to an important advantage of correlational analysis—it takes into account all available information by making direct use of the responses of *all* individuals, not just the scores of the high and low subgroups.

But the use of all available information may not be a great advantage in many practical instances. Edwards (1957) doubts whether correlational methods would order items in terms of differentiability in a substantially different way than the critical ratio. He argues that the original criterion of internal consistency may prove to be a sufficient form of item analysis. This conclusion receives partial support from Likert's original work in which he compared the two types of item analysis, finding they led to a similar evaluation of his scale items. As he concluded:

> The relation between the order of excellence for the different statements as determined by [correlation] analysis and the criterion of internal consistency as expressed by rho is +.91 [Murphy and Likert, 1938: 288].

Both forms of item analysis, however, do not *necessarily* lead to the same conclusion.

Having applied both types of item analysis to the data, one is in a position to decide whether to retain individual items. As we have said, if an item is undifferentiating, it does not contribute to the scale composed of the rest of the items and should be eliminated as a result. Thus, those items that have low item-to-total correlations and those that do not discriminate between groups with extreme attitudes should be dropped from the final scale. Likert (1932) provides some of the reasons why a statement may fail to perform according to original expectations:

(1) The statement may involve a different issue than the one involved in the rest of the statements. . . .
(2) The statement may be responded to in the same way by practically the entire group. . . .
(3) The statement may be so expressed that it is misunderstood. . . .
(4) It may be a statement concerning fact which individuals who fall at different points on the attitude continuum will be equally likely to accept or reject.

Dropping one or more items that fail to discriminate involves modifying not only the measurement instrument but perhaps also the conceptualization about what that instrument is in fact measuring. Items retained in the scale should be compared with items that are discarded. If the discarded items failed to differentiate for the second, third, and/or fourth reasons suggested by Likert, then the original conceptualization of the attitude may be retained. If the discarded items are different in content, however, a reconceptualization of the attitude represented by the remaining items is in order (Scott, 1968). This redefinition should distinguish the attitude from that measured by the discarded items.

Assessing a Likert Scale

After choosing items to comprise the final scale, one might assume the rest of the process would be straightforward. Simply add up an individual's response to each of the items. The total is assigned to the respondent as a scale score. But at least two questions must be answered first. What form of the individual item should be summed? Second, what is the reliability of the final scale? The importance of the second question is demonstrated by asking a third (rather facetious) question—who would want a scale that is unreliable, that is, primarily composed of random rather than systematic variation? Obviously no one, hence the importance of the second question. The first two questions are related the reliability of the scale is influenced by the choice of a weighting scheme to combine the individual items.

Most simply, scale scores may be computed by summing the response scores of the component items with the responses given the following integral values for favorable statements: strongly agree a value of 4, agree 3, undecided 2, disagree 1, and strongly disagree 0. The weighting scheme is reversed for unfavorable statements so that higher scores always indicate more favorable attitudes toward the object or phenomenon. In most instances, this summation of raw scores in which each item is scored identically and each item contributes equally to the total scale score is perfectly adequate. Nunnally (1978: 606) argues for such parsimonious treatment of component items for two reasons. He finds it difficult to defend other arbitrary systems of weighting in comparison to an equal-weighting scheme. He also finds little gain from the effort: unweighted and weighted summative scores regularly correlate quite highly. This conclusion echoes the results of Likert's original attempt to devise a complex scoring procedure based on the normal distribution. Sewell (also see Alwin, 1973) arrived at the same conclusion:

> The problem of assigning weights to items in a scale is one which is rather annoying but not of great practical significance in light of the roughness of most sociometric devices at the present time. Several studies have shown that essentially the same final results are obtained with arbitrary common sense weighting as with more complicated, but still arbitrary, statistical techniques [Sewell, 1941: 284; 289].

How should we interpret individual scores on the final scale? Likert's procedure is not concerned with the location of individual items on an underlying attitude continuum. Consequently, one cannot provide an absolute interpretation of a respondent's score in terms of that continuum. While the researcher can make the statement that a score falling at one extreme value of the scale (0) is an unfavorable attitude and that a score of the opposite extreme (40 for a 10-item scale) is a favorable one, the interpretation of scores falling between these possible extremes is very difficult. For example, if the research is designed to assign individuals to the class of those for or against a particular attitude object, this procedure will not do.

The difficulty stems from the fact that the interpretation of a score on a summated scale is not independent of the distribution of scores of the group of respondents (Edwards, 1957). Responses labelled "favorable" and "unfavorable" are defined relative to a particular group. This point is implicit in Likert's discussion of test standardization:

> It is certainly reasonable to suppose that just as an intelligence test which has been standardized upon one cultural group is not applicable to another so an attitude scale which has been constructed for one cultural group will hardly be applicable in its existing form to other cultural groups [Likert, 1974: 242].

In other words, the interpretation of scores falling between the extremes is problematic except in relative terms. The "neutral" point on the continuum is not known. There is no evidence to suggest that it corresponds to the midpoint of the scale values. However, interpretation of scale scores may be made relative to the mean as suggested by Edwards:

> If we use the mean of the group as our point of origin, then each of the individual attitude scores can be expressed as a deviation from this origin. We assume that the mean represents the typical or average attitude of the group. Then scores that are higher than the mean can be interpreted as scores that are more favorable than the average for the group and scores that are lower than the mean can be interpreted as scores that are less favorable than the average [Edwards, 1957: 158].

The score of any individual relative to the group mean may be expressed as a simple arithmetic difference between the individual's attitude score, X_i, and the group mean, $\overline{X}$: $x_i = X_i - \overline{X}$. Usually, however, we would like to know how far from the mean x_i is relative to everyone else in the group. This is because the value of a distance on an attitude scale often has little meaning without some frame of reference. For example, we cannot tell how deviant an individual is if we only know that she is -2.5 scale units less than the mean on Adorno's Fascism scale. However, if we also know the percentage of the sample at each scale value, we can judge the extremity of her response. The traditional way to do this is to convert the difference scores, x_i, into z scores by dividing each x_i by the standard deviation of the sample. A z score indicates how many standard deviation units an individual is from the group mean. If the standard deviation of the sample of respondents to the Fascism scale is 2.5, then our individual with the deviation score of -2.5 has a z score of -1.0. If the scale scores are approximately normal, we would then realize about 84% of the sample reported greater attraction to totalitarian beliefs than our hypothetical respondent.

Finally, the researcher needs to assess the reliability of the summated scale. The reliability of linear composites is treated in greater detail in Carmines and Zeller (1980). Here we briefly mention the two reliability coefficients that have received the most attention—the split-half and alpha estimates.

The split-halves method, also known as the Spearman-Brown prophecy formula after its creators, was Likert's choice as a reliability estimate given the minimum computational effort required to generate it. To compute the split-half reliability, the total set of items is first divided into halves. Next, scores on both halves are correlated to obtain estimates of the reliability of each half. The total set of scale items, however, is twice as long as each half. Therefore, the reliability of the total scale is computed using the Spearman-Brown prophecy formula:

$$\rho_{xx}'' = 2\rho_{xx}' / 1 + \rho_{xx}' \qquad [2]$$

where ρ_{xx}'' is the reliability of the scale and ρ_{xx}' is the correlation between halves of the scale. While computationally simple, the split-halves method is not without certain drawbacks. Most important, different reliability coefficients may be obtained with each of the different possible ways of splitting the set of scale items into two equal groups. Faced with this indeterminacy, Cronbach (1951) developed coefficient alpha that provides a unique estimate of reliability based upon the interitem correlation matrix:

$$\alpha = N\bar{\rho} / [1 + \bar{\rho}(N-1)] \qquad [3]$$

where N is equal to the number of items and $\bar{\rho}$ is equal to the mean interitem correlation.[8] Today, alpha is preferred as an estimate of scale reliability.

There is one more question to be asked concerning the final scale. Does it measure what it is supposed to measure? This question relates to the *validity* of the scale. There are a number of ways to answer this question. Unfortunately, none of them is conclusive. We do not deal with the question of scale validity here. (See Carmines and Zeller, 1980, and Sullivan and Feldman, 1980, for detailed discussions of different types of validity relevant to multiple-item measurements.)

Criticisms of Likert's Approach

There are several limitations involved with Likert's original criteria for evaluating the unidimensionality of a set of items. Here, we will deal with two specific problems with the approach—selection of items and selection of item weights. Likert scaling treats each item as a separate predictor of the respondent's total score. Consequently, the types of item analysis he proposes (here we will concentrate on the correlational method)[9] focus on how strongly the item is related to the total scale score. However, since the total includes the item as a component, a correlation between the two will be artificially inflated because both the item and the total score contain the item's variance. A more appropriate test would be to examine the relationship between the item and the scale without the item. A correction formula was originally offered by Peters and Van Voorhis (1940)[10]:

$$r_{i(T-i)} = (r_{iT}\, \sigma_T - \sigma_i) / \sqrt{(\sigma_T^2 + \sigma_i^2) - 2r_{iT}\, \sigma_T \sigma_i} \qquad [4]$$

where r_{iT} is the correlation between item and total score, σ_T is the standard deviation of the total score, and σ_i is the standard deviation of the item score.

The greater the number of items in a scale, the less each will contribute to the variance of the scale and, consequently, the less bias will be introduced by each item. This correction may, however, have important consequences for scales composed of a few items, as individual items make up a far greater proportion of scale score variance.

Yet, this procedure is not sufficient to guarantee a unidimensional scale. In certain instances, item analyses are quite deceptive. Substantial item-to-scale (corrected) correlations are often considered sufficient evidence that the items are measuring a single, common phenomenon. This evidence, however, is far from conclusive. It is possible, for example, that two or more approximately equal and independent subsets of items are contained within the scale.[11] In this situation the corrected item-to-total correlations would suggest that the items are measuring a single phenomenon—that the scale items are unidimensional. While each item would correlate significantly with the total scale, this would be due to the fact that the item is only related to a subset of the total items in the scale. Such clusters of items should be identified and scaled separately. Both the validity and the reliability of a scale might be seriously reduced by combining unrelated sets of items based on correlational methods of item analysis.

What can be done to improve the quality of Likert scales? Visual inspection of the interitem correlation matrix may reveal highly related subsets within the item pool as well as indicators that do not relate to any other items. Eyeballing a matrix for clusters is a rather imprecise process, however. A more effective technique specifically designed to answer the question of the dimensionality of multiple-item summative scales is factor analysis. As we will see, however, even sophisticated factor analyses may not always provide definitive answers to questions of dimensionality.[12]

An Example of Likert Scaling: The Rosenberg Self-Esteem Scale

A large-scale study of the development of political orientations and behavior during adolescence provides the data base from which we will draw a series of items to scale according to Likert's criteria. The data consist of a stratified random sample of 1,000 high school seniors from 25 public schools in Pennsylvania. The students were personally interviewed during April and May 1974 by trained interviewers from the Institute for Survey Research at Temple University. Each interview lasted approximately 50 minutes.

The interview and questionnaire elicited information concerning each adolescent's opinions toward the political system and various citizenship roles, his or her participation in a wide range of conventional political activities, as well as the respondent's level of political information and various demographic characteristics. Also included were numerous survey items designed to measure a variety of personality traits. One of these traits, the respondent's self-esteem, was measured by a set of 10 items originally constructed by Milton Rosenberg (1965: 305-307). The linear composite formed by summing the responses to each of these items is appropriately named the Rosenberg Self-Esteem Scale. It is these data that we analyze below to determine their unidimensionality and fit to the Likert model.

The 10 items that compose the Rosenberg Self-Esteem Scale are found in Table 1. Each is a statement about the respondent's positive or negative feelings regarding him or herself. Each respondent is permitted to choose one of five possible responses—almost always true, often true, sometimes true, seldom true, never true. The items are scored such that the response presumed to be indicative of the highest level of self-esteem is scored 5 while the lowest self-esteem response is 1. While these items were scored by the researcher on an a priori basis, positive and negative responses to each item might have been determined by the various item analysis methods discussed earlier. If we had no justification for a priori scoring of items, we could have scored all items in the same manner and reflected items, 2, 4, 6, 7, and 9 (or alternatively, 1, 3, 5, 8, and 10) after noting their negative correlations with the other items. It is important to note the direction of item reflection for interpretation of the final scale. If all items had been scored in reverse of the way they are presented in Table 1, a high value on

TABLE 1
Self-Esteem Items (N = 943)

		Response Frequency	Response Percentage
SE1:	I feel that I have a number of good qualities.		
	(5) almost always true	150	16
	(4) often true	456	48
	(3) sometimes true	321	34
	(2) seldom true	13	1
	(1) never true	3	0
SE2:	I wish I could have more respect for myself.		
	(1) almost always true	71	8
	(2) often true	233	25
	(3) sometimes true	362	38
	(4) seldom true	217	23
	(5) never true	60	6
SE3:	I feel I'm a person of worth, at least on an equal plane with others.		
	(5) almost always true	328	35
	(4) often true	399	42
	(3) sometimes true	189	20
	(2) seldom true	24	3
	(1) never true	3	0
SE4:	I feel I do not have much to be proud of.		
	(1) almost always true	18	2
	(2) often true	54	6
	(3) sometimes true	152	16
	(4) seldom true	402	43
	(5) never true	317	34
SE5:	I take a positive attitude toward myself.		
	(5) almost always true	228	24
	(4) often true	387	41
	(3) sometimes true	249	26
	(2) seldom true	67	7
	(1) never true	18	1

TABLE 1 (Continued)

		Response Frequency	Response Percentage
SE6:	I certainly feel useless at times.		
	(1) almost always true	15	24
	(2) often true	116	41
	(3) sometimes true	396	26
	(4) seldom true	338	7
	(5) never true	78	1
SE7:	All in all, I am inclined to feel that I am a failure.		
	(1) almost always true	7	1
	(2) often true	25	3
	(3) sometimes true	104	11
	(4) seldom true	348	37
	(5) never true	459	49
SE8:	I am able to do things as well as most other people.		
	(5) almost always true	195	21
	(4) often true	502	53
	(3) sometimes true	225	24
	(2) seldom true	18	2
	(1) never true	3	0
SE9:	At times I think I am no good at all.		
	(1) almost always true	5	1
	(2) often true	33	3
	(3) sometimes true	183	19
	(4) seldom true	394	42
	(5) never true	328	35
SE10:	On the whole, I am satisfied with myself.		
	(5) almost always true	298	32
	(4) often true	420	45
	(3) sometimes true	181	19
	(2) seldom true	34	4
	(1) never true	10	1

the Self-Esteem Scale would indicate a lack of self worth. As coded, however, a high scale score is associated with high personal esteem.

Can these 10 items be combined into a single scale? Alternatively stated, do these 10 items measure a single attitude as required by summative scaling? The results of two principal types of item analysis are presented in Table 2.

Likert's criterion of internal consistency, a difference of mean's approach to an item's discriminatory power, and the critical ratio test, a more exact difference of means test, are presented for each of the 10 self-esteem items in Table 2. These tests are based on groups of high and low scores each comprising about 22% of the total sample. The difference between the mean scores of each of these two extreme groups on each item is found in column 3. This difference of means corrected for the distribution of responses to each item (the critical ratio or t test) is presented in column 5. To simplify evaluation, the quality of each item as determined by its rank on each test is also found in this table (columns 4 and 6).

The data presented in Table 2 show considerable consistency in the results obtained by the two methods of analysis for evaluating the ability of items to discriminate among respondents. Depending on the particular test, item 2 or 8 provides responses least consistent with the rest of the scale. Item 5 is the most discriminatory item according to both difference of means tests. The correlation between the rankings also indicates basic congruence in results between these two methods: the Spearman's rho equals .775.

Correlational methods of item analysis are also presented in Table 2. Column 7 contains item-to-total correlations for each of the 10 self-esteem items. This procedure produces rankings identical to the critical ratio test. Item 2 has the weakest while item 5 has the strongest relationship with the total scale. But as we noted earlier, this item-to-total correlation (as well as both difference of means tests) is biased because the particular item contributes to the total scale score. Consequently, we recomputed each of the item-to-total correlations after eliminating the ith item from the scale in the calculation of the ith item-to-scale correlation. The corrected coefficients are presented in the ninth column of the table. In this example, little difference appears in the rank ordering produced by the two correlational methods (Spearman's rho = .97). However, the weakness of the second item is further highlighted by the corrected item-to-total correlation. This similarity among methods may not occur in all instances. It will depend upon the number of items in the scale, the amount of variance each item contributes to the scale, and the existence and relative size of clusters of items within the scale.

TABLE 2

Item Analysis of Rosenberg's Self-Esteem Scale (N = 943)

Item	Mean	Discriminatory Power	(Rank)	Critical Ratio	(Rank)	Item to Total Correlation	(Rank)	Corrected Item to Total Correlation	(Rank)
SE1	5.78	1.18	(9)	20.06	(7)	.614	(7)	.519	(6)
SE2	2.96	1.36	(8)	15.03	(10)	.512	(10)	.533	(10)
SE3	4.09	1.40	(5)	22.78	(5)	.651	(5)	.550	(5)
SE4	4.00	1.57	(3)	22.13	(6)	.632	(6)	.508	(7)
SE5	3.80	1.76	(1)	27.01	(1)	.707	(1)	.635	(1)
SE6	3.37	1.39	(7)	19.85	(8)	.606	(8)	.489	(8)
SE7	4.30	1.48	(5)	24.70	(2)	.682	(2)	.586	(2)
SE8	3.92	1.13	(10)	18.37	(9)	.562	(9)	.457	(9)
SE9	4.07	1.51	(4)	23.46	(4)	.663	(4)	.572	(3)
SE10	4.02	1.58	(2)	24.63	(3)	.664	(3)	.571	(4)

TABLE 3
Correlation Matrix of Rosenberg Self-Esteem Scale (N = 943)

	SE1	SE2	SE3	SE4	SE5	SE6	SE7	SE8	SE9	SE10
SE1	1.000									
SE2	.158	1.000								
SE3	.463	.220	1.000							
SE4	.502	.288	.296	1.000						
SE5	.407	.293	.422	.348	1.000					
SE6	.234	.285	.245	.319	.370	1.000				
SE7	.332	.216	.359	.450	.359	.385	1.000			
SE8	.388	.134	.417	.246	.354	.213	.313	1.000		
SE9	.325	.245	.335	.368	.386	.457	.509	.243	1.000	
SE10	.401	.212	.429	.295	.487	.285	.410	.382	.383	1.000

Finally, it is important to note the different results obtained by the various methods of item analysis. The rank-order correlation between the least powerful test of item discrimination—the simple difference of means test—and the most powerful one—the corrected item-to-total correlation—is only .65. Only one item is ranked similarly by these two methods. These results suggest that social scientists should not rely on only one method of item analysis, but should use several in assessing a particular scale.

Based upon the above analyses, the second item appears to be the weakest in the scale. Is this a single weak item? Are we missing item clustering by the analysis techniques used to this point? Examination of the interim correlation matrix (Table 3) clearly reveals the weakness of item 2. All nine correlations between the item and the rest of the components of the self-esteem scale are substantially below the average interitem correlation. But whether distinct clustering of items is present is more difficult to discern. An elegant answer to this question is provided by a factor analysis of the interim correlation matrix.

Table 4 contains a single-factor solution for the self-esteem items. The inferences drawn from this analysis seem to corroborate the earlier item analyses. Factor loadings for all items with the notable exception of item 2 are greater than .5. This solution explains approximately 40% of the variance shared by these items.

These data, however, do not conform perfectly to a one-factor model.[13] The initial analysis revealed two factors with eigenvalues greater than 1.0.

TABLE 4
Factor Analyses of the Rosenberg Self-Esteem Items (N = 943)

	One Factor Solution		Two Factor Solution				
	Factor Loadings	Communality	Unrotated Factor Matrix		Varimax Rotated Factor Matrix		Communality
	F1		F1	F2	F1	F2	
SE1	.585	.342	.594	-.265	.608	.232	.423
SE2	.379	.144	.378	.155	.158	.377	.167
SE3	.618	.381	.629	-.279	.643	.248	.474
SE4	.552	.305	.552	.169	.272	.510	.334
SE5	.667	.444	.660	-.065	.513	.421	.440
SE6	.529	.280	.542	.313	.163	.604	.391
SE7	.650	.423	.652	.184	.332	.591	.459
SE8	.518	.269	.528	-.282	.573	.173	.358
SE9	.631	.398	.643	.276	.260	.649	.490
SE10	.644	.415	.643	-.148	.559	.349	.435

Could there be some clustering of items we had missed earlier? Table 4 also contains both the unrotated and rotated two-factor solutions. The rotated solution identifies two clusters of items—the first cluster comprised of items 1, 3, 5, 8, and 10; the second items 2, 4, 6, 7, and 9. While mathematically appropriate, we could determine no substantive interpretation for this pattern. We returned, therefore, to the unrotated solution for clues. Factor 1 of this solution is essentially equivalent to the one factor solution presented in Table 4, while the second factor reveals five items with negative factor loadings. These items are precisely those that had the highest loadings on factor 1 of the rotated structure. It turns out that this pattern of positive and negative loadings on the second factor of the unrotated solution corresponds to the pattern of positive and negative wording of the self-esteem items. That is, returning to Table 1, we see that items 1, 3, 5, 8, and 10 ask the respondent to judge "good" qualities while the rest of the items ask for self-evaluations of "bad" qualities. Thus, we interpret the second factor as a response set factor, not as a substantively different dimension.

Conclusion

The summated rating scale is ubiquitous in the social sciences. Its popularity is based on two primary considerations: the simplicity of the procedures involved in constructing a summated scale and the very permissive assumptions that underlie this scaling model. After items have been selected for the scale, the computation of the scale scores for a group of respondents could hardly be simpler: Sum the responses given to all items. The method does not require judges nor does it assign scale values to individual items as does Thurstone scaling.

While elaborate procedures have been developed for differentially scoring individual responses and unequally weighting items in the final scale, the conventional approach of scoring responses identically using successive integers (assuming the items have an equal number response categories) and having each item contribute equally to the total scale score can be justified on two grounds. First, as noted, the procedure is simple to apply and straightforward in its logic. Second, various methods of constructing summative scales generally correlate quite highly with one another (Alwin, 1973). On the other hand, optimally weighted scales often have higher reliabilities than their equally weighted counterparts (Greene and Carmines, 1979; Zeller and Carmines, 1980; Carmines and Zeller, 1980). In many situations, however, the difference in reliabilities is not substantial. As a consequence, the conventional approach will be adequate for most theoretical and practical applications in the social sciences.

As we have seen, the summated model is based on three major assumptions—that each item has a monotonic trace line, that the sum of the item trace lines is monotonic and approximately linear, and that the set of items measures only the attribute of interest. Only the last assumption tends to be somewhat problematic. It is difficult to determine conclusively that the items as a whole are measuring only a single phenomenon. This limitation is not as serious as it may appear at first glance, however, since many separate, partial pieces of evidence often indicate that the individual items can be combined into a single score without the loss of much important information. In the end, the summated model is widely used because, as Nunnally (1978: 84) aptly states, it "makes sense and works well in practice."

Appendix

Each of the procedures discussed in this chapter is readily accessible to both students and researchers via many available program packages. With SPSS, the T-test, Reliability, and Factor subroutines provide all of the computations required for any of the topics of item analysis described previously.

T Test: Subprogram for Comparison of Sample Means. This subprogram calculates both the difference of means and the critical ratio tests. Furthermore, it provides a statistical test of the difference between extreme group variances and an estimate of the significance of the critical ratio if extreme group means are not equal. The necessary SPSS control cards are:

(1) Recode: Scale (1st quartile = 1) (2nd & 3rd quartile - 2) (4th quartile = 3)

(2) T Test Group = scale (1, 3) Variables = items in scale

The recode card is necessary to identify the extreme groups for this difference of means test.

Reliability: Subprogram for Item and Scale Analysis. This subprogram, not included in the second edition of the SPSS manual, but now distributed with version 7.0 SPSS, computes all correlational item analyses and various scale reliability coefficients. The reliability analysis procedure card is specified as follows:

(1) Reliability Variables = variable list / Scale (label) = variable list / Model - alpha

(2) Statistics 1, 3, 4, 8, 9

where
1 = item means and standard deviations
3 = interitem correlation matrix
4 = scale mean and variance
8 = mean, variance, maximum, minimum interitem correlations
9 = item-to-total statistics
   a. scale mean of item deleted
   b. scale variance of item deleted
   c. corrected item-total correlations
   d. squared multiple correlations between items and total
   e. alpha if item deleted.
Reliability coefficient based on raw scores as well as standardized scores are output.

Factor: Subprogram for Factor Analysis. This subprogram produces a wide variety of factor-analytic solutions. The user should be familier with the basic issues raised by Kim and Mueller (1978a, 1978b) prior to analysis.

The procedure cards necessary to produce the basic information discussed in our scaling example are:

(1) Factor   Variables = items in scale
(2) Statistics   2, 4, 5, 6

where
2 = correlation matrix
4 = communalities, eigenvalues, proportion of variance explained
5 = initial factor solution
6 = rotated factor solution.

4. AN INTRODUCTION TO GUTTMAN SCALING

Historically, Likert scaling developed as a response to the deficiencies attributed to the earlier techniques of Thurstone. Likewise, Guttman scaling, the subject of this chapter, developed as a critical alternative to both of these earlier methods of attitude scaling. In particular, Guttman argued that neither Likert's nor Thurstone's techniques conclusively established that a series of items belong on a *unidimensional* continuum. Evidence that each item is a part of a single underlying dimension, he insisted, is provided by a scale's ability to predict responses to all of its component items on the basis of total scores. This is contrary to the usual intentions of researchers employing item analysis procedures to build a scale; that is, items are chosen for their ability to predict a total score. As we shall discuss in greater detail later, this dispute over the relative merits of the various scaling models largely turns on different conceptions of dimensionality. For now, however, let us introduce Guttman's method of scaling.

Guttman scaling, also known as scalogram analysis and cumulative scaling, is a procedure designed to order *both* items and subjects with respect to some underlying cumulative dimension. It is a deterministic model of scaling; each value is a single-valued function of the underlying continuum (Guttman, 1944: 176).[14] It is in terms of this functional relationship that Guttman defines a scale:

For a given population of objects, the multivariate frequency distribution of a universe of attributes will be called a *scale* if it is possible to derive from the distribution a quantitative variable with which to characterize the objects such that each attribute is a simple

TABLE 5
A Perfect Guttman Scale

	Items						
Subjects	1	2	3	4	5	6	Scale Score
A	1	1	1	1	1	1	6
B	1	1	1	1	1	0	5
C	1	1	1	1	0	0	4
D	1	1	1	0	0	0	3
E	1	1	0	0	0	0	2
F	1	0	0	0	0	0	1
G	0	0	0	0	0	0	0

function of that quantitative variable. Such a quantitative variable is called a scale variable [1950: 64].

A perfect Guttman scale is depicted in Table 5. From each subject's scale score (Guttman's "quantitative" or "scale" variable) we can accurately predict the subject's response to each of the dichotomous items that make up the scale. A score of three, for example, indicates a positive response to items 1, 2, and 3 rather than any other three items. Similarly, a score of one indicates an affirmative response only to the first item. But, if another subject H had answered only item 2 positively, we would no longer have a perfect scale for we cannot accurately predict responses to the individual items given only a knowledge of scale scores. Both F and H would receive scale scores of one even though their responses to individual items differ. These two response patterns cannot be accommodated on the same Guttman scale.

A perfect relationship between scale score and item score (as depicted in Table 5) is rarely if ever achieved. Scalogram *analysis* anticipates that the ideal deterministic model will be violated. The question becomes one of the degree of deviation one is willing to tolerate before it is established that the model fails to serve as an adequate representation of the empirical data. The primary purposes of this chapter are to define deviations from a perfect scale, discuss various criteria for evaluating the degree of deviation, and show how these criteria are used to judge the scalability of a set of items.

Assessment of Error

We define error simply as the deviation of the observed response pattern from the ideal pattern required by the cumulative model. It is assumed that the amount of deviation, or error, observed is strictly a function of the failure of items and subjects to conform to Guttman ordering procedures. Thus, when a set of data exhibits *less* than a specified proportion of errors, it is concluded that the data can be represented on a cumulative scale—an underlying dimension, representable by a single quantitative variable. Each item and each subject has a unique meaning in terms of its location on this dimension. However, a wide variety of manipulations exists that make it possible to alter the proportion of error in the data relative to the model.

The two predominant forms of error counting are: minimization of error (Guttman, 1947, 1950; Chilton, 1966, 1969; Green, 1956) and deviation from perfect reproducibility (Goodenough, 1944; Edwards, 1948). A comparison of these two procedures will allow for a more complete investigation of their properties and applications.

According to minimization of error, the number of errors is the least number of positive responses that must be changed to negative or negative responses that must be changed to positive in order for the observed response to be transformed into an ideal response pattern. The results of this procedure are displayed in Table 6, which depicts all possible response patterns and error counts for a four-item Guttman scale.

A contradiction exists between the procedure for counting errors Guttman suggests and the theory of scalogram analysis he develops. The problem makes itself most evident in the following statement:

> Each member of the population will have one of these values assigned to him. This numerical value will be called the person's score. From a person's score we would then know precisely to which problems he knows the answers. *Thus a score of 2 does not mean simply that the person got two questions right, but that he got two particular questions right, namely, the first and second. A person's behavior on the problems is reproducible from his score. More specifically, each question is a simple function of the score* [Guttman, 1950: 66; emphasis added].

The number of positive responses to items is not merely a count of answers given in the affirmative. Rather, it is an assessment of the location of subjects with regard to the proposed cumulative continuum. Consequently, errors as defined by the minimization of error criteria may undercount locational errors by focusing on errors in positive or negative responses.

TABLE 6
Two Forms of Error Assignment for a Four-Item Guttman Scale

Response Pattern				Assignment of Error Guttman	Edwards-GE
* +	+	+	+	0	0
* +	+	+	-	0	0
+	+	-	+	1	2
* +	+	-	-	0	0
+	-	+	+	1	2
+	-	+	-	1	2
+	-	-	+	1	2
* +	-	-	-	0	0
-	+	+	+	1	2
-	+	+	-	1	2
-	+	-	+	2	2
-	+	-	-	1	2
-	-	+	+	2	4
-	-	+	-	1	2
-	-	-	+	1	2
* -	-	-	-	0	0

*Indicates Ideal scale pattern.

An example will help to clarify this point. If the response pattern (- + + -) is observed, then according to the above statement the fact that the subject scored positively on two items suggests the ideal response pattern (+ + - -). The minimization of error technique described above would count the observed pattern as reflecting one error; the first negative response needs to be changed to a positive one in order to transform the response pattern to the ideal pattern (+ + + -). However, according to the interpretation that Guttman himself places on the scale score, the observed response pattern actually reflects two errors. For if the ideal pattern for two positive items is (+ + - -), and the observed pattern is (- + + -), the minimum number of signs which must be changed to complete the transformation is in fact two. Thus, the cumulative assumption on which a Guttman scale is based is inconsistent with the minimization of error criterion. In such a case, the scale variable loses the most important component of its interpretation.

Guttman fails to address himself to this apparent inconsistency. Edwards (1948), however, derived an error-counting procedure based on the initial assumption that items should in fact be perfectly reproducible from a subject's responses. As Edwards elaborates:

> The suggestion offered here is that we, for a given sample, assume perfect reproducibility, and make our predictions of item responses on this assumption. Error may then be measured in terms of the number of responses departing from the patterns predicted. Cutting points for items would thus be rigorously defined and would always occur between ranks. *Scores which are inconsistent with the assumption of perfect reproducibility would be scored as the nearest scale type consistent with the notion of a scale* [1948: 318; emphasis added].

The technique that Edwards asserts is "consistent with the notion of a scale" is exactly that procedure that Guttman referred to when discussing the intended interpretability of two positive responses; assigning ideal response patterns to subjects on the basis of the number of items scored positive (Guttman, 1950: 66). This error-counting procedure, which we will refer to as the Goodenough-Edwards technique, is also presented in Table 6. While error counting based upon deviations from perfect reproducibility will result in a greater number of errors than minimization of error, this is an accurate description of the data based upon scalogram theory. It is for this reason that the deviations from perfect reproducibility method for counting errors is superior to the minimization of error method.

Scale Construction

Let us begin the discussion of scale construction with the simple case of a set of data that conforms perfectly to the cumulative model. The procedures described will also serve us in the more complex case of non-perfect fit discussed shortly. The data matrix of interest is a subject by stimuli arrangement of responses as shown in the top section of Table 7. Note that we are dealing only with dichotomous responses; that is, each subject is permitted only one of two judgments with respect to each stimuli—favorable (1) or unfavorable (0). Focusing on either one or the other response categories (in Table 7, we focus on favorable responses), compute the number of such responses for each individual and the proportion of such responses to each stimuli for all individuals. For example, subject A responds favorably a total of four times and two-thirds of the

TABLE 7
Construction of a Simple Error-Less Scale

I. Initial Data Matrix

		Stimuli				
Subjects	1	2	3	4	5	
A	0	1	1	1	1	4
B	0	0	1	0	1	2
C	0	0	0	0	1	1
D	1	1	1	1	1	5
E	0	0	0	0	0	0
F	0	1	1	0	1	3

.17 .50 .67 .33 .83

II. Translation of Stimuli (Columns)

		Stimuli				
Subjects	5	3	2	4	1	
A	1	1	1	1	0	4
B	1	1	0	0	0	2
C	1	0	0	0	0	1
D	1	1	1	1	1	5
E	0	0	0	0	0	0
F	1	1	1	0	0	3

.83 .67 .50 .33 .17

III. Translation of Subjects (Rows)

		Stimuli				
Subjects	5	3	2	4	1	
D	1	1	1	1	1	5
A	1	1	1	1	0	4
F	1	1	1	0	0	3
B	1	1	0	0	0	2
C	1	0	0	0	0	1
E	0	0	0	0	0	0

.83 .67 .50 .33 .17

subjects respond favorably to stimuli 3. Enter these calculations at the margins of the data matrix.

Having accomplished this preliminary task, two more steps are needed. First, interchange the columns of the matrix so that the stimuli are arranged from the highest to lowest proportion of positive responses. This task is shown in the second part of Table 7. Second, arrange the rows of the data matrix so that the subjects are ranked from the greatest number of favorable responses to the fewest. Completion of these two steps (which may be done in either order) will provide the triangular pattern evident in cumulative scales. (See the bottom of Table 7.)

Perfect scales are not often observed. Consequently, we need some means of handling data that do not fit the triangular pattern as well as some measure of the fit between the cumulative model and the empirical data. Two principal techniques of scale construction have been proposed (although there are many variations): the Cornell technique for scale analysis (Guttman, 1947) and the Goodenough-Edwards technique (Edwards, 1957). In each case the error-counting procedure which is employed has been discussed, and it now remains to integrate this procedure with the additional elements of the method.

The Cornell technique for scale analysis is essentially an extension of the minimization of error criterion to a series of observed response patterns. Cutting points are established on the basis of minimization of error, with the only condition being that no item category possess more error than nonerror. The ordering of items on the underlying continuum is likewise a function of minimization of error among the observed responses. As such, the Cornell technique takes advantage of inversions in the ordering of items based upon decreasing marginal probabilities in order to achieve the highest possible reproducibility. The reliance of the Cornell technique on empirical manipulations of data confine the interpretation of scale results. The item ordering and scale scores may be a function of random errors in the data rather than the construct underlying responses to scale items. Consequently, the final scale may be a sample specific result that is neither representative of the population nor replicable in other samples.

In contrast, the Goodenough-Edwards technique for scale analysis is based upon two closely related principles which are consistent with scale theory: (1) the predicted ideal response pattern for a subject is a direct function of the number of items the subject responded to positively and (2) errors are assigned on the assumption of perfect scale reproducibility (Edwards, 1957: 187). Application of these principles insures that cutting points are established objectively and that their placement is consistent with subject response shifts and the resulting rank order.

Beyond its greater theoretical plausibility, the Goodenough-Edwards technique also has some practical advantages. Scale analysis is based on observed responses rather than inferred responses derived under the minimization of error procedure. Consequently, the simple translation of rows and columns described in identifying a perfect scale is appropriate here as a first step prior to error counting.[15]

Following the construction of a proposed scalogram by either method, it is necessary to establish if in fact the scale possesses the theoretically required properties of a cumulative scale.

Every test of scalability is at least partially grounded in the theoretical premise that the observed subject response pattern is a single-valued function of a quantitative scale variable. Since it is accepted that a perfect correspondence between scale variable and observed response pattern is rarely achieved, it is necessary to have a measure that reflects the extent to which the observed response patterns are identical to the predicted ideal response patterns. Guttman originally proposed a statistic, the coefficient of reproducibility (CR), to assess the degree of scalability of empirical data:

> The amount by which a scale deviates from the ideal scale pattern is measured by a coefficient of reproducibility. This coefficient is simply a measure of the relative degree with which the obtained multivariate distribution corresponds to the expected multivariate distribution of a perfect scale. It is secured by counting up the number of responses which would have been predicted wrongly for each person on the basis of his scale score, dividing these errors by the total number of responses and subtracting the resulting fraction from one [Guttman, 1950: 77].

The formula for this coefficient may be expressed as follows:

$$CR = 1.0 - (\text{\# errors})/\text{total responses} \qquad [5]$$

$$= 1.0 - (\text{\# errors})/[(\text{\# items}) \times (\text{\# respondents})]$$

It is obvious that the method of error counting will have a direct affect on the value of CR.

CR, calculated according to the requirements of the particular scale construction technique, is a measure of goodness of fit between the observed and the predicted ideal response patterns. As a result of error considerations, each scaling technique measures CR in a different fashion. Guttman's original formulation will be referred to as CR_{error}, since errors are counted following the successive application of all possible minimizations of error. The CR associated with the Goodenough-Edwards method will be referred to simply as CR_{ge}.

As we have pointed out, scalability is a function of the extent to which observed response patterns can be accurately reproduced on the basis of assigned quantitative scale scores. Guttman established the standard that a set of items should be considered scalable if the observed error in reproduction equals 10% or less of the total responses. However, Guttman's measurement of error was inconsistent with the proposed cumulative interpretation of scalogram theory. As a direct result, CR_{error} fails to reproduce the originally observed response patterns within the stated limits of accuracy (Edwards, 1957: 184).

This does not prove to be the case when error is counted by the Goodenough-Edwards method. With this technique, error is assigned to every observed response which fails to correspond to the ideal scale pattern predicted by the total scale score. The result is that CR, calculated using the Goodenough-Edwards concept of error, accurately reflects the degree to which observed response patterns deviate from ideal response patterns. Retaining Guttman's original specification that a scale is interpretable if it reflects 10% or less error, the scalability criterion now becomes $CR_{ge} \geq .90$. Of course, this is a more conservative test of scalability than that which employs CR_{error}.

The Goodenough-Edwards CR, because of its error-counting procedure, protects against the possibility of a *spuriously* high level of reproducibility. However, it is still true that items with extreme marginal distributions will tend to inflate the value of CR_{ge}. As a safeguard against this possible occurrence, Edwards (1957) suggests comparing CR_{ge} to the minimal marginal reproducibility (MMR).

The calculation of MMR is based on the fact that an item's reproducibility can be no less than the proportion of responses in its modal category.[16] As such, the total reproducibility can be no less than the sum of the proportion of responses in the modal category for each item in the scale, divided by the number of items. This value, MMR, reflects the reproducibility of a series of items *based only upon knowledge of the item marginal distributions*. As an example, consider the marginals for positive responses to four items in Table 8. The marginal probabilities of .8, .6, .4, and .2 (found in row 5) are associated with modal probabilities of .8, .6, .6, and .8. In this case,

$$MMR = (.8 + .6 + .6 + .8)/4 = .7$$

TABLE 8
Comparison of MMR for Various Marginal Distributions
of a Four-Item Scale

1	2	3	4	MMR
.50	.50	.50	.50	.50
.60	.60	.40	.40	.60
.70	.50	.50	.30	.60
.70	.70	.30	.30	.70
.80	.60	.40	.20	.70
.80	.80	.20	.20	.80
.90	.70	.30	.10	.80
.85	.85	.15	.15	.85
.90	.90	.10	.10	.90
.95	.85	.15	.05	.90
.95	.95	.05	.05	.95

If the observed marginals were .95, .85, .15, and .05, MMR would equal .90. Thus, the value of MMR is a function of extreme marginals.

The requirements for scalability based upon MMR are as follows: (1) the MMR must not be so large that it is assumed that CR_{ge} is strictly a product of extreme item marginals and (2) the difference between CR_{ge} and MMR must be of such a magnitude that it is possible to attribute an improvement in the prediction of response patterns based upon scalogram analysis.

The relationship between CR and MMR can be illustrated as follows:

$$CR = (TR - SE)/TR \qquad [6]$$

$$MMR = (TR - ME)/TR \qquad [7]$$

where

TR = total responses
SE = scale errors
ME = marginal errors, the sum of all nonmodal frequencies.

The difference between the two coefficients is

$$CR - MMR = [(TR - SE)/TR] - [(TR - ME)/TR] \qquad [8]$$

$$= (ME - SE)/TR$$

In words, the difference between these coefficients is a function of the improvement in prediction provided by the scale over the marginal frequencies of individual items. This difference ranges from 0 (if the scale provides no improvement of prediction) to ME/TR (if the scale fits the Guttman criteria perfectly). Given that the maximum marginal errors in any item that can occur are 50%, this difference has a theoretical maximum of .50. The maximum that will occure in any sample is a function of the item marginals.

Interpreting the difference between CR and MMR on a scale from 0 to ME/TR can be difficult. As a consequence, various alternatives have been suggested. For example, Menzel (1953) also noticed that CR would be necessarily high if item marginals were substantially skewed regardless of any relationship among the items. He argued that the number of scale errors attributable to each item cannot be higher than the frequency of responses to the nonmodal category. Consequently, the maximum number of scale errors is the sum of the responses to the nonmodal category of each item. Menzel designed the coefficient of scalability (CS) as a measure of a scale's ability to predict item responses in comparison to predictions based on marginal frequencies. The formula for CS is:

$$CS = 1.0 - (\text{scale errors}/\text{marginal errors}) \qquad [9]$$

Todd (1974) suggests that CS is easily interpretable as a proportional reduction in error (PRE) statistic[17]:

$$CS = (ME - SE)/ME \qquad [10]$$

As a measure of improvement in fit, CS provides fixed reference points. If scale predictions are perfect (i.e., there are no scale errors), CS = ME/ME = 1.0. If the scale provides no improvement in prediction (i.e., scale errors equal marginal errors), CS = 0. Menzel suggests a coefficient of .60 is an indication of scalability. This is, however, only a rule of thumb; a CS of .60 has no explicit theoretical justification.

The final criterion for scalability involves analysis to insure against the presence of a second scale variable (i.e., a second underlying scalable dimension). Setting the minimum acceptable value of the coefficient of reproducibility at .90 means that 10% error can be tolerated while the data are considered scalable. Scalogram analysis, however, assumes the presence of only one underlying scalable dimension. If a particular *error* response pattern is observed frequently in the data, this is an indication that the data should be represented by more than a single dimension (Guttman, 1947: 457). Thus, in order to establish that a set of items is scalable, it is necessary that observed error responses be essentially random, thereby providing no evidence of a second underlying dimension.

In summary, the Goodenough-Edwards technique for scale analysis stipulates three necessary criteria which must be fulfilled in order that a series of ordered items be considered scalable. The first, similar to Guttman's procedure, is that the coefficient of reproducibility, CR_{ge}, be greater than or equal to .90. Second, the MMR must not be excessively high, and the difference between CR_{ge} and MMR must indicate that some improvement in scalability is realized as a function of knowledge of total scores. And finally, those response patterns which reflect error must be nonsystematic in character.

Assignment of Scale Scores

The final step in scale analysis is the assignment of scale scores to subjects. The assignment of scale scores would be straightforward if only perfect scales were observed; the quantitative variable would be equal to the number of positive responses. For example, an observed response pattern (+ + + − −) is assigned the scale variable "3." The number 3 allows the inference that the subject not only responded positively to three items, but that these three items were *the first three*.

The problem arises when nonscale responses are assigned ideal predicted response patterns and scale scores are assigned according to these ideal patterns. If the response pattern (− + + − −) is observed, there is no number from 0 to 5 which accurately locates the respondent on the underlying scale continuum. However, nonscale responses do occur, and the researcher is faced with the problem of what score to assign so that interpretation of the scale will be least affected. This assignment problem, as we shall see, is in fact a pseudo-problem, based upon minimization of error scale construction techniques.

Two predominant forms of scale score assignment have been developed for scales constructed through minimization of error techniques: (1) assignment based upon nearest ideal predicted response pattern and (2) assignment based upon the number of positive responses. To differentiate between these procedures, assume that for a five-item scalogram, one response pattern is observed to be (− + + − −). Based upon the minimization of error assessment of nearest ideal scale type, the response pattern would be reclassified as the pattern (+ + + − −) and assigned the scale variable 3. However, because there are only two pluses in the original observed pattern, the number of positive responses method assigns the scale variable 2.

This lack of correspondence between observed response pattern and either scale score procedure introduces a serious restriction on the interpretation of scale results for subjects who display nonscale responses. Equally as damaging is the case where an observed response pattern could technically be assigned to two or more ideal predicted types. The researcher, in trying to decide which ideal pattern the observed response is actually a deviation from, is forced to make an ambiguous assignment as to how the subject should be characterized with regard to the scale attribute. For the observed response pattern (− + − + −), the ideal predicted response patterns based upon minimization of error could be either (+ + + + −), (+ + − − −), or (− − − − −). Scale score assignment based upon nearest ideal type is either 4, 2, or 0, depending upon the choice of the researcher. Scale score assignment based upon the number of positive responses observed in the original pattern is again equal to 2.

The assignment of scale score problem illustrated above is a pseudo-problem once the presence of a scalogram is established by the recommended criterion that CR_{ge} be greater than or equal to .9. When a scale has been constructed in this manner, rather than by minimization of error techniques, the assignment of scale scores based on the nearest ideal type is identical to the assignment of scale scores in accordance with the number of positive responses. The assignment of scale scores to subjects is not an issue when the Goodenough-Edwards procedures have been employed, because the number of positive responses is identical to the nearest ideal scale type. This method of score assignment is also much easier to use. In summary, scale construction and scoring methods based on the perfect reproducibility model is preferred to the minimization of error approach.

The calculation of scale scores for the cumulative scale by summing the number of positive responses sounds as if it is the same scoring rule used in summative or Likert scales. In fact, the assignment procedure is identical. The distinction between the cumulative and summative models rests in *when* the responses are totaled and how this total is interpreted. Scale scores are assigned to respondents only if all (or at least a substantial subgroup) of their responses fit the model being considered. Guttman scale scores are assigned only when CR is greater than .90, for example. Likert scores are computed only if the item-to-total correlations are statistically significant and greater than the interitem correlations. It is certainly possible for data to fit one model and not the other or that neither model is appropriate.

The interpretation of total scores distinguishes these two scaling models. A Likert score of 2, for example, means that the respondent replied favorably to *any* 2 of n stimuli. An individual who responds positively to two items out of n that compose a Guttman scale has responded to two *specific* items, the two that are the "easiest" or "most acceptable" to the group of respondents.

Guttman Scaling and Item Analysis

Edwards (1957: 172) argues that scalogram analysis is not strictly a method for constructing or developing an attitude scale. Rather, it is a process by which it is determined whether a series of items and a sample of subjects conform to a specified set of criteria designated as the requirements of a Guttman scale. To this point we have treated Guttman scaling from this perspective. That is, Guttman scaling has been discussed from a hypothesis-testing standpoint.

Yet the cumulative scaling model has also been used as an exploratory technique for selecting items that conform to scale criteria from a larger set of items. This selection process occurs quite frequently and is in large part a function of our inability to establish the homogeneous content of a series of items prior to scaling. One method of item selection that has proved useful is the examination of bivariate relationships among all items using a correlational model that is consistent with the cumulative assumption of Guttman scaling.

The bivariate relationships between responses to the components of a four-item Guttman scale are shown in Table 9. (Here we are dealing with a perfect scale.) The four items partition the population into five groups, those individuals that do not accept any items (n_5), those that accept only item 1 (n_4), and so forth. In order to be consistent with the cumulative model, the relationship between any two items must be a weak monotonic relationship. That is, low responses may be paired; high responses may be paired; a high response on one variable may be paired with a low response on another, but not vice versa. Those conditions are maintained in each of the 2×2 components of the large matrix of relationships in Table 9.

What correlation coefficients are appropriate measures of weak monotonic relationships? Several are available. Torgerson (1958) suggests tetrachoric r. Robinson et al. (1968) offer Yule's Y as an alternative. Yule's Q has perhaps been most frequently used. MacRae (1970) has demon-

TABLE 9
Item Analysis and Guttman Scaling*

I	II	III	IV		
0000 ↓	1000 ↓	1100 ↓	1110 ↓	1111	– response pattern
n_5	n_4	n_3	n_2	n_1	– population

Item 4 is accepted by n_1 respondents.
Item 3 is accepted by n_1+n_2 respondents.
Item 2 is accepted by $n_1+n_2+n_3$ respondents.
Item 1 is accepted by $n_1+n_2+n_3+n_4$ respondents.

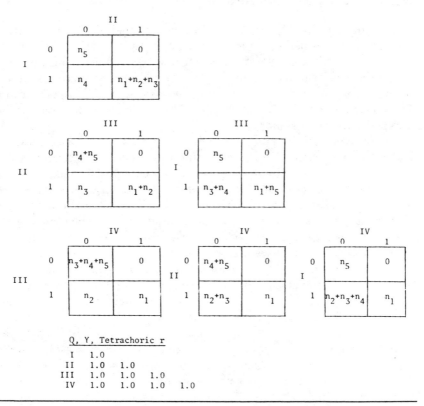

Q, Y, Tetrachoric r

I	1.0			
II	1.0	1.0		
III	1.0	1.0	1.0	
IV	1.0	1.0	1.0	1.0

*Adapted from Torgerson, 1958.

strated its considerable value in the study of congressional voting by analyzing large numbers of roll call votes. All of these coefficients reach maximum values of 1.0 under conditions of weak monotonicity.[18] If the relationships are not weakly monotonic, the coefficients will all have different values with Q being the largest. Magnitude of relationship as a selection criterion has largely been ad hoc. MacRae and others who use this technique examine alternative cutoffs in attempting to find the most theoretically plausible cluster of items. In other words, ad hoc cutoffs exist to serve the researchers' purposes. Cutoffs of .9 or .8 for Yule's Q are most common.

Senate Voting—The Structure of Support
for a Consumer Protection Agency
(An Example of Guttman Scaling)

In 1975, the U.S. Senate made its fourth attempt in 5 years to establish a federal consumer protection agency (Agency for Consumer Advocacy; ACA) to represent consumer interests before other federal agencies and courts. As conceived by its sponsors, the new agency would not be able to issue regulations on its own, but would petition other federal agencies to do so. The ACA would also be charged with gathering information of interest to consumers.

Fourteen roll call votes were taken on S200 and proposed amendments (see Table 10). Sponsors were able to turn back most of the attempts to weaken the legislation with one exception. An amendment (offered by Senator Dole) to prevent the ACA from participating in federal proceedings on agricultural issues was accepted by a 2-1 margin (CQ181).

The question we pose is whether the Senators were expressing some unidimensional attitude in voting on the amendments to S200. In asking the question this way, we initially eliminate the two votes CQ171 and CQ184, the vote on cloture and the final passage vote. While these two votes fit our final scale, they were removed from our analysis to ease interpretation of the results of our scaling efforts. Thus, our set of roll calls for analysis are the 12 substantive amendments to S200. Opponents of this legislation attempted to amend the bill to include many exceptions. Consequently, a final scale might be interpreted as a ranking of roll calls supporting special interests. Alternatively, the liberal position is support for the original bill, that is, for a viable and general consumer protection agency.

The correlations among the 14 roll call votes are presented in Table 11. We can see immediately that CQ169 (an FCC exception) does not appear related to the rest of the roll call votes. In addition, CQ181 (the Dole Amendment exempting farm issues) is not related to a number of the other votes. These same conclusions may be drawn from an initial Guttman scale of these 12 roll calls. CQ169 and CQ181 contribute a majority of the scale errors (38 of 104 or 37%). Finally, the scale does not meet our evaluative criteria (CR =. 874).

TABLE 10

Senate Roll Call Votes on S200, a Bill to Establish an Agency for Consumer Advocacy (ACA)—May 1975

CQ169 Magnuson amendment to add a provision that would prohibit the ACA from intervening in the broadcast license proceedings of the FCC (Adopted 69-21).

CQ170 Weicker amendment to delete a provision in the bill that would prevent the ACA from intervening in labor-management disputes (Rejected 37-51).

CQ171 Ribicoff motion to close further debate (Adopted 71-27).

CQ174 Johnson amendment to limit the ACA's authority to seek judicial review of other agencies' actions to cases that affect consumer health or safety (Rejected 29-63).

CQ175 Helms amendment to require the ACA to notify everyone against whom a consumer complaint has been lodged and that these complaints be made public (Rejected 41-50).

CQ176 Pearson amendment, in the form of a substitute bill, to set up an Office of Consumer Counsel in each of 24 major federal departments and agencies (Rejected 22-70).

CQ177 Taft amendment to permit the ACA to intervene in NLRB proceedings dealing with secondary boycotts and jurisdictional strikes (Rejected 36-57).

CQ178 Ribicoff motion to table the McClure amendment to prohibit the ACA from intervening in federal procedings with the intention of limiting the sale, manufacture, or possession of firearms (Rejected 27-67).

CQ179 Taff amendment, in the form of a substitute bill, to set up an Office of Consumer Affairs in the executive branch and corresponding offices in other federal departments and agencies (Rejected 28-64).

CQ180 McClellan amendment to replace the single ACA administrator with a three-member commission appointed by the President with Senate Confirmation (Rejected 40-48).

CQ181 Dole amendment to prevent the ACA from intervening in federal proceedings directly affecting producers of livestock, poultry, or agricultural commodities (Adopted 55-34).

CQ182 Scott amendment to authorize the Justice Department to control ACA litigation instead of leaving it to ACA's attorneys (Rejected 24-67).

CQ183 Griffin amendment, in the form of a substitute bill, to delete all provisions except the requirement that federal agencies prepare cost-benefit assessments on proposed regulations (Rejected 24-66).

CQ184 Passage of S200, a bill to set up an independent Agency Consumer Advocacy to represent consumer interests before other federal agencies and courts, and to gather and disseminate consumer information (Passed 61-28).

TABLE 11
Correlations Among Roll Call Votes (Yule's Q)

CQ#													
169	100												
170	79	100											
171	19	93	100										
174	05	.93	99	100									
175	21	90	100	100	100								
176	-26	85	94	98	94	100							
177	75	100	96	95	91	84	100						
178	-08	77	100	100	95	83	79	100					
179	14	95	99	100	100	97	97	100	100				
180	15	83	100	98	94	96	85	94	97	100			
181	-51	93	91	86	69	77	31	70	84	83	100		
182	24	89	98	98	100	92	88	86	97	93	59	100	
183	19	93	100	99	100	89	97	100	99	100	91	97	100
184	19	91	99	98	100	91	94	100	100	100	84	86	100	100

A scale of the remaining 10 roll call votes provides an acceptable scale by most criteria (CR = .923, MMR = .645, CS = .782). Furthermore, no error patterns predominate. However, the data permit us to illustrate the construction of a "contrived" item, that is, a combination of responses to a subset of items. The roll calls on CQ170, 177, and 180 all fall at approximately the same point on the scale. This is also the location of many of the scale errors. We might argue that there are no real differences between these roll calls and that inconsistent votes are random errors that should be ignored. We combine items as follows: one or fewer positive responses are coded as a no response to the contrived item; two or more positive responses are coded as a yes response. The combination of two of these items (CQ170, 177) also makes some intuitive sense in that they deal with a common exception—labor-management disputes.

The final scale (Table 12) is a minimal improvement over the 10-vote scale (CR = .9433, MMR = .6650, CS = .8308). Over 78% of the Senators fit one of the nine perfect scale patterns. The exemption most supported by the Senators was denial of control over firearms. The alternative least supported was Senator Pearson's alternative that the ACA be scrapped for internal consumer advocates in each of the federal departments.

There is an epilog: Advocates of the bill did not rejoice at the passage of S200 for long. While the House approved the creation of a consumer protection agency late in the year, the slim margin of victory (208-199) disappointed supporters of this legislation. With so little support in the House

TABLE 12
A Guttman Scale of Senate Voting

CQ vote	178	185	180 187 190	184	189	192	193	186	
scale score									
8	1	1	1	1	1	1	1	1	- Case, Hart (P), Humphrey, Inouye, Jackson, Pastore, Proxmire, Ribicoff, Williams, Mondale, Nelson, Pell, Brooke, Percy, Cranston, Stevenson, Glenn, Hart (G)
7	0	1	1	1	1	1	1	1	- Bentsen, Burdick, Cannon, Church, Magnuson, Mansfield, Moss, Muskie, Scott (H), Schweiker, McIntyre, Eagleton, Clark, Huddleston, Leahy
6	0	0	1	1	1	1	1	1	- Byrd (R), Montoya, Randolph, Stafford, Abourezk
5	0	0	0	1	1	1	1	1	- Roth, Chiles, Stone
4	0	0	0	0	1	1	1	1	- Domenici
3	0	0	0	0	0	1	1	1	
2	0	0	0	0	0	0	1	1	
1	0	0	0	0	0	0	0	1	- McClelland, Byrd (H), Scott (R), Allen, Helms
0	0	0	0	0	0	0	0	0	- Curtis, Eastland, Griffin, Hruska, Thurmond, Young, Fannin, Tower, McClure, Hansen, Bartlett, Garn

Error Patterns

	178	185	190	184	189	192	193	186	
7	1	1	0	1	1	1	1	1	- Hathaway, Weicker
7	1	1	1	1	1	1	1	0	- Pearson
6	0	0	0	1	1	1	1	1	- Hatfield, Hollings, Haskell
5	1	0	1	1	1	1	1	1	- Fong
4	1	1	0	1	1	1	1	1	- Packwood
4	0	0	1	1	1	1	1	1	- Sparkman
3	0	0	1	0	1	0	1	1	- Stevens
2	0	0	0	0	0	1	1	1	- Stennis
2	0	0	1	0	0	0	1	0	- Dole, Brock
1	0	0	0	0	0	0	0	1	- Talmadge
1	0	0	0	0	0	1	1	0	- Taft
1	0	0	0	0	0	1	0	0	- Nunn

	178	185	190	184	189	192	193	186
% Support	29	52	56	67	69	71	72	75
# Errors	4	3	8	1	1	7	3	7

58

and under the threat of a veto from President Ford, the sponsors in both houses decided against convening a conference to consider the differences between the House and the Senate bills.

Participation in Politics—A Cumulative Scale?

Students of politics have noted that persons who engage in one political act often participate in other acts. Milbrath (1965) argues that involvement in politics is structured in a certain way: Participation is hierarchical. This hierarchy of political acts is organized such that individuals who perform acts at the top of the hierarchy also perform acts lower in the hierarchy. Individuals at the bottom of the hierarchy, however, perform only the lowest ranking (most frequent) political acts.

The logic underlying this argument goes something like the following. Political participation may be ranked hierarchically in terms of the personal commitment (defined as time, energy, and money) required for each act. The apathetic citizen invests little in the political world and receives little in return. Voting is routine. It is the easiest way for many citizens to act politically. Many other political activities, however, are available to citizens. They may discuss politics with family and friends. This discussion can be carried to the point of attempting to persuade others to accept a point of view. Citizens can express their opinions publicly. This may be done passively by displaying campaign buttons and bumper stickers or actively by discussion with strangers. Citizens can invest more time and effort in politics by contacting local and national public officials, contributing to campaigns, and attending political meetings and rallies. Finally, citizens may participate by working in campaigns, soliciting funds, or even running for and holding public office.

Milbrath's hypothesis that political participation is hierarchically structured is equivalent to the hypothesis that political acts would conform to a Guttman scale. This scale of political acts is portrayed in Table 13. Initial empirical support for this scale consisted of aggregate frequencies of occurrence. Voting is the most frequent political act. Membership in a political party is the least common one.

The cumulative scale in Figure 1 implies more than the ranking of actions by aggregate proportions of the populations so engaged. The scale implies particular constraints on *individual* behavior. Citizens who joined political parties have also performed all other political acts. If citizens perform only one political act it is voting. Individuals involved in four political acts participate in four *particular* acts—no action higher on the hierarchy than wearing a campaign button will be undertaken.

Does individual behavior fit the constraints of the cumulative scale? Verba and Nie (1972) suggest that participation by American citizens is

TABLE 13
Milbrath's Hierarchy of Political Involvement—A Hypothesized Guttman Scale

Citizens	Vote-Natl Elections	Vote-Local Elections	Attempt to Persuade Others	Wear a Campaign Button	Attend Rallies	Contact Public Officials	Contribute Money	Join Political Party	Scale Score
Politically Active (Hi)	1	1	1	1	1	1	1	1	8
	1	1	1	1	1	1	1	0	7
	1	1	1	1	1	1	0	0	6
	1	1	1	1	1	0	0	0	5
	1	1	1	1	0	0	0	0	4
	1	1	1	0	0	0	0	0	3
	1	1	0	0	0	0	0	0	2
	1	0	0	0	0	0	0	0	1
Politically Apathetic (Lo)	0	0	0	0	0	0	0	0	0

not hierarchically structured. Empirical evidence provided by a national survey of political behavior suggests that the Milbrath hypothesis is not supported:

> Researchers simply may have overestimated the degree of structure in and the amount of correlation among the varieties of participatory acts when interpreting simple frequency distributions [Verba and Nie, 1972: 40].

Verba and Nie discovered that 53% of their respondents participated in none of the six most difficult political acts. If these data were to fit the cumulative model, however, 80% of the population should not have performed any "difficult" political acts (as only 20% of the population participated in the "easiest" of the six political acts). Political activity is not cumulative, according to Verba and Nie, but is a multidimensional phenomenon with several factors influencing the participatory behavior of American citizens.

Congressional voting and political participation are just two subjects where cumulative scaling have been applied. Guttman's procedures have been used extensively in the construction of attitude indices by social scientists (see D. Miller, 1970, and Robinson et al., 1968) But while the technique was designed as a means to examine the dimensionality of a series of qualitative responses to attitude surveys, scaling has been used by many social scientists to answer a variety of research questions. Anthropologists have employed Guttman scaling in their studies of cultural evolution (Carneiro, 1962) and development in rural communities (Young and Young, 1962). Sociologists have applied analysis to the study of bureaucratic structures (Udy, 1958), leisure activities (Allardt et al., 1959), evolution of legal institutions (Schwarts and Miller, 1962), sexual experiences (Podell and Perkins, 1957), and neighboring activities (Wallin, 1953). Political scientists have found cumulative scaling a useful technique for examining political development (Snow, 1966), international conflict and cooperation (Moses et al., 1967), political violence (Nesvold, 1971), and congressional (e.g., Rieselbach, 1966; MacRae, 1970; Clausen, 1973; Weisberg, 1974) and judicial decision making (e.g., Schubert, 1968; Spaeth, 1969).

In this chapter we have provided a brief overview of Guttman scaling. The simplicity with which we have described this procedure is, unfortunately, not an adequate summary of the technique. Almost all aspects of Guttman scaling from its goodness of fit tests to its conclusiveness as a measure of unidimensionality have been subjected to many criticisms, some of which we will discuss in the next chapter.

5. ISSUES IN GUTTMAN SCALING

In the preceding chapter we provided a brief introduction to the mechanics of building a Guttman scale. Here, we extend the discussion a bit further taking into account both practical and theoretical issues that have been raised by those who have used Guttman's methods to identify unidimensional scales. In particular, we will discuss: (1) some of the solutions that have been offered for dealing with problems of too much data (i.e., too many respondents or too many stimuli), (2) missing data problems, (3) how polytomous items can be analyzed, (4) additional perspectives on scale errors and how they affect coefficients of reproducibility, and (5) a recently proposed test of scalability.

Too Many Respondents/Too Many Items

Too much data is often a "problem" in scale analysis. Yet as Clausen and Van Horn (1977) suggest, it is a problem only in the "technological sense that most computer programs have limited capacities." Too much data can often be used by researchers to improve their scales. We shall now review many of the methods used to reduce the analyzed data matrix to a manageable size and explain how some of these methods may be valuable aids to better scale development.

How extra data are treated depends upon the purposes underlying scale development. Will the researcher use the scale to distinguish among a particular set of stimuli or to identify differences between respondents with respect to the scaled stimuli? Is the researcher concerned with the possibility of measurement error? (Could random error be the reason the data do not fit a scale?) Has a particular sample of respondents or stimuli been chosen? Must all data be included in the final scale? Some of these questions were considered by Guttman and his colleagues. Others have arisen in more recent years as researchers pushed this methodology and available computer software to their limits.

The "Contrived-Item" Technique. What can be done if our data fail to meet the standards of the Guttman model? Stouffer et al. (1952) show that reproducibility can be improved under certain circumstances. If the stimuli to be scaled are all part of the same theoretical universe of content, but at the same time are not important individually, it is possible to create "contrived items" by combining responses to two or more items. Items that are combined are those that fall at approximately the same position on the scale. (We have already seen items combined this way in the scaling of Senate roll call votes in the previous chapter.) Each individual's "response" to a contrived item is determined on the basis of his or her responses to all items that make up the new contrived variable. Stouffer et al. refer to this as the H-Technique.

The H-Technique has several purposes. In creating a contrived item, we are often eliminating idiosyncratic (nonscale) responses within the cluster of items being combined by using the responses to all of the items to determine the individual's most likely position at that point on the scale. Idiosyncratic responses may be due to random measurement error or due to the effect of another variable on responses to the items (systematic variance or nonrandom measurement error).

The H-Technique was originally devised to improve reproducibility. It can, however, be used simply to consolidate data before analysis begins. Items, assuming common content, may be combined on the basis of item marginals. If, for example, three items are used to create one new item, the data matrix will shrink by 2n, where n is the number of respondents. This approach also attempts to correct data for error. Stricter criteria for scale evaluation should be used if data are being manipulated prior to analysis.

The "Contrived Respondent" Technique. A method designed to improve scale reproducibility without discarding items or combining several items has been proposed by Alexander and Perry (1967). They suggest that since the attitudes of groups rather than particular individuals are often of interest, the unique response patterns of individuals need not be preserved. Consequently, we can create a contrived respondent in much the same way that we created a contrived item. Individuals with the same total score can be combined into a single contrived respondent by assigning the predominant response of the group members to be the contrived response to each item.

This technique was originally designed to improve the fit between the data and the cumulative model. It can, however, be used to pare down the size of the data matrix prior to evaluating model adequacy.

Other Solutions. Clausen and Van Horn (1977) discuss a series of practical solutions to "too much" data:

(1) Eliminate items with extreme marginals. These items provide very little information about whether they belong in any given scale. (In other words, items with extreme marginals can be added to many different data sets without increasing the number of scale errors significantly.)
(2) Eliminate items that have marginals similar to items retained in the scale.

(3) Sample items. Use the maximum number permissible by available computer software. (Stratification is preferable if certain characteristics of the items are important to research aims, but appear infrequently in the population.)

(4) Retain only "significant" items—depending on some external judgment of significance.

(5) Analyze subsets of content or behavior as determined by external criteria such as time or location.

Clausen and Van Horn believe all of these solutions are deficient because they throw away valuable data. They argue that all data should be retained for analysis with the "extra" data serving to test the reliability of resultant scales. Guttman scaling has often been used to identify the dimensions of congressional voting. Clausen and Van Horn ask, How can we analyze 500 to 600 items per Congress? They proceed by identifying broad clusters of common content among roll calls, for example, economic policy, civil rights and liberties, foreign and defense policies, and social welfare. Each cluster is divided randomly into two samples. Next, they identify subclusters of common content through factor analyses of the two samples of each issue cluster. Scales are created in each sample based on the results of the factor analyses. An intersample, interscale correlation matrix is then computed and examined to determine the similarity of scales. Their empirical results suggest that an assumption of dimensional equivalence across samples is not always valid—several scales identified in one sample do not appear to have counterparts in the second group of roll call votes. This process, advocated by Clausen and Van Horn, both reduces the size of the item clusters analyzed and provides some evidence of the stability of the scale in multiple samples.

Each of these solutions is of some use in reducing the size of the data matrix being analyzed. Each has disadvantages. All are ad hoc. All need to be guided by theoretical understanding of the phenomena under study to avoid biasing the final scales.

Missing Data

An infrequently discussed but important problem facing users of this technique is what to do about missing data. Missing data is a nasty little problem that arises in most empirical research when the subjects of research are so inconsiderate as to fail to supply the social scientist with all the information he or she would desire. It often forces the user of a statistical methodology to develop some ad hoc procedure in order to prevent losing some data that have been collected. Because they could not escape the problem of missing data or entice their subjects to supply them with additional information, researchers using Guttman scales have developed their own rules of thumb to guide analysis of data with missing values.

One set of criteria for handling missing data that focuses on the characteristics of an individual's response to all of the scale items is suggested by Anderson et al. (1965):

(1) If the respondent fails to offer a position on 50 percent or more of the scale items, do not assign a scale position, i.e., list as "not classified."

(2) If the respondent fails to offer a position on less than 50 percent of the scale items (i.e., answers more than 50 percent of all items), all possible scale types should be determined and the average scale score assigned to the respondent. If the respondent falls halfway between two scale types, assign the respondent to the scale position closest to the median of the scale.

Some variations on these simple rules seems to be followed by most social science researchers (although in many cases exactly how missing data problems are handled is not reported). More complex schemes exist to attempt to predict missing responses from observed responses and/or additional information. In most cases, the complexity and arbitrariness of such schemes seems to overwhelm any benefits derived from their use.

Readers who remember the scale of senators voting on the proposed consumer protection agency discussed in Chapter 4 may now wonder what we did with missing data in building that scale. Only 73 senators are listed in Table 12. For simplicity, we removed all senators who failed to vote on each of the 10 roll calls included in the scale. Now we can examine the response patterns that contain missing data.

Table 14 contains the voting records of all of the senators who failed to vote on at least one of the roll calls. Following the rules specified above, we did not classify five senators: Bayh, Hartke, Buckley, Goldwater, and Gravel. Each of these individuals voted only four or fewer times when the roll was called. For each of the others, we note the possible scale scores for the respondent, their scale score(s) if they voted in accordance with the identified dimension, their average score, and their score closest to the scale median (6) if their average fell halfway between two scale scores.

Polytomous Items

Guttman argues that the techniques of scalogram analysis are equally amenable to items with any number of response categories. His theoretical

TABLE 14
Missing Data in Senate Roll Call Votes on S200

178	185	180 187 190	184	189	192	193	186	Number Missing	Possible Scale Score	Scale Score if Perfect	Average Scale Score	Scale Score Closest to Scale Median	
1	1	1	1		1	1	1	1	7-8	8	7.5	7	-Kennedy
1	1		1		1	1		3	5-8	8	6.5	6	-Mathias
1	1		1	1			1	3	5-8	8	6.5	6	-Tunney
1	1		1	1	1	1	1	1	7-8	8	7.5	7	-McGovern, Culver
	1		1	1			1	4	4-8	7,8	NC	NC	-Bayh
	1		1		1	1		4	4-8	7,8	NC	NC	-Hartke
0	1		1	1	1	1	1	1	6-7	7	6.5	6	-Symington, Biden, Bumpers
0	1	1	1	1			1	2	5-7	7	6		-McGee
0	1	1		1			1	3	4-7	7	5.5	6	-Metcalf
0		1		1	1	1	1	2	5-7	6,7	6		-Ford
0	0		1	1	1	1	1	1	5-6	5,6	5.5	6	-Morgan
0	0			1	1	1		3	3-6	4-6	4.5	5	-Long
0	0	1	0	1			1	2	3-5	---	4		-Johnston
0		0		0	1	1	0	2	2-4	---	3		-Beall
0	0	1	0	0	1		0	1	2-3	---	2.5	3	-Baker
0	0		0	0	1	0	0	1	1-2	---	1.5	2	-Bellman
					0	0		6	0-6	0,1	NC	NC	-Buckley
0	0		0	0	0	0	0	1	0-1	0	0.5	1	-Laxalt
0				0	0	0		4	0-4	0,1	NC	NC	-Goldwater
								8	0-8	0-8	NC	NC	-Gravel

NOTE: NC = Not classified.

examples encourage researchers to scale items where subjects respond to items with more than two categories. Yet in applying scalogram techniques empirically,

It has seldom been found that an item with four or five categories will be sufficiently reproducible if the categories are regarded as distinct. One reason for this is the verbal habits of people. Some people may say "Strongly Agree" where others may say "Agree," whereas they have essentially the same position on the basic continuum but differ on an extraneous factor of verbal habits. By combining categories, minor extraneous variables of this kind can be minimized. By examining the overlapping of (responses) within the columns of each question, it can be determined how best to combine the categories so as to minimize the error of reproducibility for the combinations [Guttman, 1947: 191].

Careful consideration of this statement reveals that Guttman is in fact discussing two independent strategies of category combination. The first is combination on the basis of verbal habits of subjects; the second, that of minimization of error.

The method of combining categories in order to raise reproducibility is known as "the method of successive approximations." Guttman and his colleagues suggest that this procedure is justified due to the differing verbal habits of subjects who share a similar position on the underlying continuum. However, combination is accomplished by observation of item category response patterns. The "verbal habits of people" remain an important criteria of combination *only until the combinations derived from such violate the minimization of error*. Then the question becomes one of appropriately combining "neutral" categories with either the most "positive" categories or the most "negative" categories to achieve the smallest number of deviations from the ideal or expected scale pattern (Suchman, 1950: 112).

Schuessler (1952) has questioned the validity of the method of successive approximations. He first instructed a sample of subjects to respond to seven items with one of three alternatives: "Agree," "Undecided," or "Disagree." Those subjects who were "Undecided" were assigned to the "Agree" or "Disagree" category in such a way as to maximize reproducibility. Category combination resulted in an empirically acceptable Guttman scale. Two days later, the subjects were instructed to react to the same items, but with only two response categories per item: "Agree" and "Disagree." Comparison of responses to the dichotomous items with the responses created by combination of categories according to the minimum error criterion were sufficiently different as to challenge the assumption that adjacent categories often reflect similar location on an underlying continuum, distinguished only by differing verbal habits of subjects.

If sound interpretation of the scale variable is a goal of scalogram analysis, and certainly we have encouraged the reader to believe so, category combination based upon the minimization of error violates this purpose. Guttman scale results must not be considered independent of the method employed to obtain them. Manipulations performed specifically to yield an empirical effect are hardly sufficient to establish the validity of a scale which is the result of these manipulations. In practice, researchers should be encouraged to report the vital information relevant to item selection and category combination, thus increasing understanding of the conclusions which are drawn.

Actually, a third reason for the combination of response categories is likely the most persuasive. Ease of interpretation of the final scale is enhanced by a reduction of item cutting points. Dichotomous items, in particular, are most easy to understand with respect to a deterministic model such as the cumulative model. Up to a certain point, an individual will agree with, or is characterized by, condition y. After that point, this individual will reject y.

For this reason, one seldom encounters items employed in scalogram analysis that are in any but dichotomous form. Rather than use nondichotomous items, researchers use various justifications for combining categories to dichotomize items. Scale purification is often accomplished by combining or eliminating items rather than manipulating cutting points.

Remember, dichotomization, as all other types of response category manipulations, will affect the interpretation of the resultant scale variable. Initially, the Guttman scale researcher must decide whether subject response will be based upon a two-category or a multiple-category level of measurement. In either case, there should be a theoretical reasoning behind the cutting point(s) which ultimately dissects the distribution of each item.

Errors—How To Interpret Them, What To Do About Them

Rarely do we find a perfect Guttman scale in real-world situations. Deviations from the cumulative model should be expected. Earlier, we discussed what constituted an error and suggested several guidelines on how much error was too much error. Having identified error responses, we would like to understand what they mean and what, if anything, might be done about them.

When the triangular pattern of responses that indicate a perfect cumulative scale is violated, one or more of the following interpretations can be adopted (Runkel and McGrath, 1972: 293-297):

(1) One or more of the assumptions underlying the Guttman model are invalid with respect to the data;
(2) The "space" in which the stimuli and respondents are located is not unidimensional; and
(3) The nonfitting cells contain error due to
   (a) respondents,
   (b) stimuli, or are
   (c) unpredictable error.

Which interpretation of error is chosen is dependent on the researcher's perspective. It may be suspected (even in advance) that the data do not meet certain of the necessary criteria. Multidimensionality may be a viable alternative interpretation of certain data. One may be methodologically predisposed to attribute random error to characteristics of the respondent or nonrandom error to characteristics of the stimuli. Informed judgment works hand in hand with statistical technique in interpreting error.

The interpretation adopted determines what might be done about the errors. If we decide the cumulative model is inappropriate for the data, there is little point in applying it further. Likewise, if we determine the data to be multidimensional, there are alternative statistical models that might be applied (Kim and Mueller, 1978a, 1978b; Kruskal and Wish, 1978). If errors are attributable to respondents or stimuli, we may use certain procedures to "purify" our scale. Certain of these have been discussed already in our discussion of too much data (see "contrived item" and "contrived respondent" techniques above).

Significance Tests for Guttman Scales—A New Approach

In our discussion of the various criteria for assessing a Guttman scale in the previous chapter, we pointed out that the lower bound on reproductibility, MMR, is a function of item marginals. It is possible, for example, that MMR approach or exceed .9 if item marginals are extreme. (Refer back to Table 8 to see when this is so.) We argued that CR must be appreciably greater than MMR to support the inference that a single dimension underlies a particular set of data.

Two questions have been asked of this strategy for assessing cumulative scales. First, how much greater must CR be to be "appreciably" greater than MMR? Second, is MMR the proper reference point for evaluating CR?

To answer the second question first, many insist that MMR is an unrealistic choice of a guideline against which CR is judged. MMR is a statement of the worst possible reproducibility for a set of items. It is, however, usually true that a set of unrelated items will have a CR greater than its MMR by chance alone. Consequently, researchers have attempted to estimate an "expected CR" based on the distributions of items that are mutually independent (Green 1954; Sagi, 1959; Schuessler, 1961; Chitton, 1966; Schooler, 1968). Expected CR for a given set of items can then be compared with the observed CR. Furthermore, the difference between these two coefficients may be subject to statistical test. The standard error of expected CR can be estimated. With this estimate, the difference between expected CR and the observed CR can be converted into a Z score. The significance level of this Z score is the measure of "appreciable" improvement of the cumulative scale over chance.[19]

Having briefly reviewed the traditional approach to testing whether a set of items fit the Guttman model, we would also suggest that this approach may be outdated in light of recent developments.

Goodman (1975) offers a new test of the scalability of a set of dichotomous items. He assumes that each individual in the population is either "intrinsically scalable" or "intrinsically *unscalable.*" Given n items, there are 2^n possible response patterns and n + 1 types of intrinsically scalable individuals. (For 4 items, there are 16 response patterns of which 5 are appropriate to the Guttman model.) Individuals with all other response patterns (there are $2^n - n - 1$ other possible patterns) are classified as unscalable. Thus, Goodman's model permits n + 2 types of individuals; n + 1 scalable types and 1 set of unscalables. It is assumed that for the intrinsically unscalable individuals, their responses to each of the items are mutually independent. The response patterns of the scalable individuals correspond to their scale type.

Those whose responses match each scale type, therefore, are from both the scalable and unscalable sets of individuals. The number who fit a particular pattern are those who fit the scale and those whose responses fall there after independent responses to each item. The object is to estimate the proportion of intrinsically scalable and unscalable respondents who fit each of the n + 2 response patterns.

If this underlying model of individual responses to the stimuli is accepted, we can use Clogg's (1977) computer program for restricted latent structure analysis to estimate the required proportions of scalable and unscalable respondents. This program, available from Clogg, is appropriate because the Goodman model of the Guttman scale is simply a special case of the latent class model which is in turn a special case of Lazarsfeld's (1950) general latent structure analysis. With these estimates we can test the congruence between the proportions of respondents in each response pattern as predicted by the Goodman model and the observed data by use of a chi-square goodness-of-fit statistic (likelihood ratio test). This chi-square statistic allows the researcher a statistical test and choice of probability levels to reject the hypothesis that the data conform to the Goodman hypothesis that a single Guttman scale underlies these data with deviations from the cumulative pattern that are random. Examples of this method for evaluating Guttman scales are provided by Goodman (1975) and Kim and Rabjohn (1980).

To summarize: One problem with the various guidelines for an acceptable Guttman scale (e.g.,, CR $>$ .9, MMR $<$ .9, CS $>$ .6) is that it is possible to satisfy these rules by chance. Satisfaction of such rules does not provide definitive evidence that the scale items are consistent with the cumulative model. Significance tests have been developed to provide additional support for the scalability of items.

Conclusion

In this chapter and the preceding one, we have attempted to provide an introduction to Guttman scaling. Some of the principal issues involved in developing an acceptable scale have been discussed in detail, others have been covered only briefly, and, finally, some have not been discussed due to lack of space. The reader intent on pursuing this topic should find Gordon (1977), Mokken (1971), Torgerson (1958), and Edwards (1957) useful. The relationship of Guttman scaling to the more general latent class model is described in Lazarsfeld and Henry (1968) with further elaborations by Goodman (1975) and Dayton and MacReady (1980).

In the next chapter we turn to a discussion of a theoretically interesting but to date underutilized approach to scaling, the unfolding model.

6. UNFOLDING THEORY

The scaling methods discussed in the three previous chapters (Likert and Guttman scaling) have been widely applied throughout the social sciences. One can easily find hundreds of substantive applications of each of these methods. Not so with the scaling model to be discussed in this chapter. The unidimensional unfolding model, introduced by Coombs (1950, 1964), has found only limited applications in the social sciences, especially outside psychology. But its infrequent use, we would argue, is not an accurate indication of the potential contributions that the unfolding model can make to an understanding of social, political, as well as psychological phenomena. On the contrary, we believe that its potential role in the social sciences is substantial and that it has been only partially realized at the present time.

The purpose of this chapter is to outline the principal features of Coombs's unfolding model. In the process, we shall illustrate some possible uses of this scaling model in the social sciences. We shall focus primarily on the underlying logic of this method, paying less attention to a variety of issues that can arise in its actual application (for a more extended discussion see Coombs, 1964: 80-139).

The Basic Model

The unfolding model is based on the analysis of preferential choice data. This type of data, as we pointed out in Chapter 1, generally involves the ranking of stimuli from most to least preferred.[20] Each individual's preference ordering is called an *I scale*. For example, let us suppose a sample of voters has been asked to rank four presidential candidates—McGovern, Humphrey, Nixon, and Wallace—from most to least preferred. Letting M represent McGovern, H Humphrey, N Nixon, and W Wallace, the I scales for three hypothetical voters might be MHNW, WNHM, and NHWM. Thus, the first voter prefers McGovern to Humphrey, Nixon, and Wallace; Humphrey to Nixon and Wallace; and Nixon to Wallace. The other two voters have different preference orderings with the second voter most preferring Wallace and least preferring McGovern, while the third voter most prefers Nixon and least prefers McGovern.

The key question posed by the unidimensional unfolding model is whether there exists a common latent attribute—referred to as *J* (Joint) *scale*—underlying the different preference orderings of a set of individuals. Can both individuals and stimuli be represented in a unidimensional space such that the relative distances between them reflect the psychological proximity of the stimuli to the individuals? Alternatively stated—can the preferences of individuals, the various I scales, be consistent with a single J scale? If so, then it is reasonable to presume that individuals are employing a common criterion in evaluating the various stimuli. If not, then two distinct possibilities exist. Perhaps individuals are responding to the stimuli in purely idiosyncratic ways. No common attributes underlie their perceptions. The other possibility is that individuals employ multiple criteria in their evaluation of the stimuli. Thus, voters might react to political candidates based on their party affiliation, ideological complexion, and personality makeup. In this case, individuals' preference orderings will *not* be compatible with a single dimension, but several underlying dimensions might provide a very adequate fit to the data. (For the development of the multidimensional unfolding model, see Bennett and Hays, 1960; Hays and Bennett, 1961; Green and Carmone, 1969).

Unfolding in a Single Dimension

The process of evaluating the consistency of the individual I scales with a common J scale is known as "unfolding" the I scales. "Unfolding" also describes geometric manipulation of each I scale from the respondent's ideal or preferred location on the J scale. This procedure is exactly comparable to the reverse process of being able to fold the J scale about the points representing the person's preferred position to form the individual's own preference ranking or I scale.

These processes are illustrated in Figure 2 (adapted from Dawes, 1972). The J scale is represented along the horizontal line. The I_1 and I_2 vertical

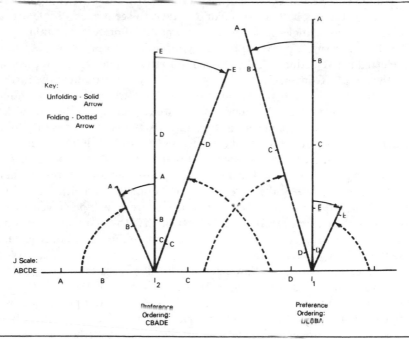

Figure 2: How I Scales Are Unfolded To Form a J Scale and How a J Scale Is Folded To Form I Scales

lines represent two preference orders—the first given by DECBA, the second by CBADE. Can these preference orders be unfolded to form a single J scale? The arrows marked unfolding show how both I_1 and I_2 can be represented on the same J scale. This J scale maintains the essential integrity of the individual I scales in the sense that a particular stimulus is closer on the dimension to a given individual than a second stimulus if and only if it is preferred to the second. For example, examining Figure 2, we see that for I_1 stimulus C is preferred over B and that on the J dimension C is closer to I_1 than is B. Similarly, again referring to I_1, D is preferred in relation to C and on the J scale D is closer to I_1 than is C. This preference-distance relationship also holds for I_2. Therefore, both of these preference orderings can be unfolded on the same dimension.

Figure 2 also illustrates how the J scale can be folded to reveal the preference orders represented by I_1 and I_2. When the J scale is folded about the ideal point representing the individual, the preference ordering may be read on the vertical scale from bottom to top. The dotted lines indicate how the J scale is folded to represent the individual I scales.

An alternative but equivalent way of demonstrating the compatibility of a set of I scales with a particular J scale is to see if each I scale can be represented as a single-peaked curve on a graph of preference rankings by the J scale. Single-peaked preference orderings imply that the more preferred a given stimulus, the closer it is to the individual's ideal position on the J scale. Conversely, the less preferred a given stimulus, the further away the stimulus is from the most preferred position. If each individual can be represented on the same J scale, we expect to see the preference functions of each decline monotonically from his or her ideal point. Figure 3 provides an example of three I scales, CDBA, ABCD, and BCAD, that are all consistent with a common J scale, ABCD. The I scale, DACB, cannot be unfolded on the J scale, ABCD. It also cannot be represented in Figure 3 as a single-peaked preference function. We can either conclude that the J scale that the other individuals share is not perceived by the person with preference ordering DACB or that this individual does not or is unable to accurately report his true preference rankings given a common J scale.

Above, we have shown how a set of individual I scales can be unfolded to form a common J scale (Figure 2). But we were only dealing with two I scales and so our task was quite simple. Given a large sample of I scales— that is, many individuals that have rank ordered multiple stimuli from most to least preferred—how can we determine whether the various preference orderings can unfold along a single dimension? Fortunately, Coombs (1964) has shown that a set of preference orderings must have certain properties for them to unfold into a common space.

An important distinction must be made initially between a *qualitative* J scale and a *quantitative* J scale. The former scale is simply an ordering of stimuli from one extreme to the other. A total of 2^{n-1} (where n is the number of stimuli) I scales will be consistent with any given qualitative J scale. Thus, a qualitative J scale of four stimuli will permit eight consistent individual preference orderings. As many as 16 I scales will be compatible with a five-stimuli qualitative J scale. A qualitative J scale is an ordinal scale, that is, we know the relative position of all stimuli on the scale, but not the distances between them.

It is possible, however, to extract additional information from rank order data. Not only do such data provide us with the necessary information to identify the relative position of all stimuli on a single scale but they also permit us to infer relative distances on this scale. Such a scale is known as a quantitative J scale. Some but not all of the distances between different pairs of stimuli on this type of scale may be ascertained (as we will demonstrate shortly). Because relative distances between stimuli are

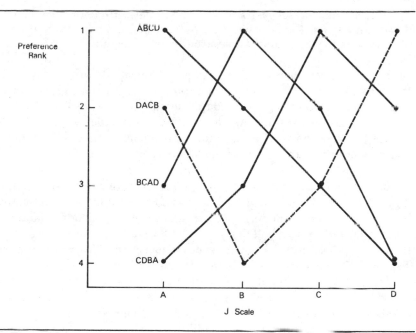

Figure 3: The Relationship Between I Scales and a Common J Scale: A Requirement of Single-Peaked Preferences

recovered, a quantitative J scale is often referred to as an "ordered metric" scale.

Each quantitative J scale will be composed of some subset of the I scales that are consistent with the same qualitative J scale. The particular subset of I scales that are offered by respondents identifies which distances are larger or smaller than others. Coombs (1964) lists the following four characteristics of a quantitative J scale:

(1) The number of distinct I scales must be no more than $\binom{n}{2} + 1$, where n is the number of stimuli.[21] Thus, for four stimuli, only seven I scales should be present.
(2) The I scales must *end* in either the first or last stimulus of the J scale.
(3) The set of I scales cannot include more than one pair of scales that are mirror images of each other. One of these I scales must begin with the first stimulus and end with the last, and the other must begin with the last stimulus and end with the first. They must be exact opposites of one another.

(4) If a complete set of I scales fit the J scale, it must be possible to arrange the I scales such that movement from adjacent scales involves the reversal of an adjacent pair of stimuli.

Next, we examine a hypothetical example of how qualitative and quantitative J scales are related to their component I scales and to each other.

Let us return to the four-candidate example we used earlier. Furthermore, let us assume that the qualitative J scale that underlies voters' preferences for these candidates is a simple liberal-conservative continuum in which George McGovern (M) is the left wing candidate, Humphrey (H) and Nixon (N) are the centrist candidates with Humphrey perceived as the more liberal, and George Wallace (W) is the most conservative candidate. Given the known relationships between quantitative J scales and individual preference rankings, we can make some predictions about the set of voter I scales that will fit the J scale. With four candidates, no more than $\binom{4}{2} + 1$ or seven I scales will be consistent with a given quantitative J scale. (2^{4-1} or 8 I scales will fit the qualitative J scale.) Second, each of the I scales observed should end with one of the extreme candidates, either M or W. We expect one pair of I scales that are mirror images of one another. If voters perceive these candidates to be located as we have suggested, then these two I scales should be opposites with one beginning with M and ending in W, while the second begins with W and concludes with M.

Table 15 presents two sets of I scales that meet all of the criteria enumerated above for a quantitative J scale, both of which are consistent with a common qualitative J scale. Four stimuli have been rank ordered by our hypothetical respondents. In this instance there are exactly seven distinct I scales in each quantitative J scale. That is, every entire set of I scales contain only two scales that are exact opposites of one another. I_1 begins with the first stimulus M and ends with the last stimulus W; I_7 begins with the last stimulus W and ends with the first stimulus M. Moreover, their preference orderings are exact reversals of each other since I_1 is MHNW and I_7 is WNHM. Finally, notice that the remainder of the I scales (I_2 to I_6) are ordered in such a way that they satisfy the condition that an adjacent pair of stimuli is reversed in adjacent I scales. For example, I_1 and I_2 are exactly the same except that the pair MH in I_1 is reversed to HM in I_2. Similarly, I_5 and I_6 have the pair HW reversed in their preference orderings. In sum, the I scales given in Table 15 meet all of the criteria necessary to be represented in a common unidimensional space.

It is important to recognize that all of these conditions must be met for the various I scales to be represented perfectly by a common J scale. Thus, preferential choice data may fail to meet the unidimensional un-

TABLE 15
A Set of I Scales and Their Common J Scales

I Scale Number	Qualitative J Scales (MHNW)	Quantitative J Scales (MHNW) I	II
1	MHNW	MHNW	MHNW
2	HMNW	HMNW	HMNW
3	HNMW	HNMW	HNMW
4	NHMW–HNWM	NHMW	HNWM
5	NHWM	NHWM	NHWM
6	NWHM	NWHM	NWHM
7	WNHM	WNHM	WNHM

I Scales that Do Not Fit Either Quantitative J Scale:

MNHW	HNWM	HMWN	WNMH
WHNM	NWMH	WMNH	MWNH
NMWH	WMHN	MWHN	WHMN
NMHW	MHWN	HWMN	MNWH

Key: M = McGovern, H = Humphrey, N = Nixon, W = Wallace

folding model for one or more of the following reasons. First, there may be more distinct preference orderings than can be represented on a single dimension. Earlier we noted that the total number of I scales that can be accommodated by a single quantitative J scale is given by the formula $\binom{n}{2} + 1$ where n is the number of stimuli. But n stimuli can be ordered in n! distinct ways.[22] For example, four stimuli can be ranked in $4! = (4)(3)(2)(1) = 24$ nonredundant ways, although only seven will fit a common J scale. Five stimuli can be ranked in $5! = (5)(4)(3)(2)(1) = 120$ different ways. But only $\binom{n}{2} + 1 = \binom{5}{2} + 1 = 5!/[(2!(5-2)!] + 1 = 11$ of these preference orderings are possible *if they are to be represented on a single scale.* Thus, actual data may fail to meet the unfolding model because there may exist preference orderings that are not assumed by a specific J scale. Second, the I scales may not end in either the first or last stimulus. Instead, an I scale may end with a "middle" stimulus. Third, the set of I scales may include more than one pair of scales that are mirror images of each other. Appearance of two or more pairs of scales that are mirror images may suggest a multidimensional preference structure. Fourth, it may be impossible to order the I scales in such a way that adjacent scales involve the reversal of an adjacent pair of stimuli. (This assumes condition 1 has not been violated, that is, that there are at most $\binom{n}{2} + 1$ I scales.) If *any* of these conditions exist, then the set of I scales cannot be unfolded to form a single J scale. That is, no common J scale can be formed such that the relative distances between the points reflect the proximity of the stimuli to each individual's ideal point. One or more individual preference orderings cannot be represented on the J scale.

As we have previously pointed out, Table 15 contains two sets of seven I scales that can be unfolded to form a single quantitative J scale. That is, these I scales meet each of the four conditions imposed by the unfolding model. Any other preference ordering cannot be represented on this scale because it would violate one or more of the four rules implied by the unidimensional unfolding model. To convince yourself that this is the case, select a preference ordering not included in the MHNW scale in Table 15 and try to unfold it on the already established J scale. No matter which I scale is chosen, the result is the same: It cannot be represented on the J scale.

Metric Information from Ordinal Data

Unfolding can provide more information than simply the relative position of the stimuli on a single dimension. Provided we are considering more than *three* stimuli, additional information about the relative distances between stimuli can be ascertained. The more stimuli, the more pieces of information about distances on the J scale can be deduced. With a four-item scale, we can determine if the distance between the two stimuli on the left end of the J scale is greater than the distance between the two stimuli on the right end. With five stimuli we can determine four more distances. In general, it is possible to get $\binom{n}{4}$ pieces of information on distances from a set of n stimuli (Torgerson, 1958), that is, we get an additional piece of information for every subset of four stimuli.[23] (Some of this information, however, will be redundant.) Because this information about distances between stimuli can be extracted from the ordinal data, the J scale is often referred to as an "ordered-metric" scale.[24]

How do we determine distances between stimuli by the unfolding method? First, we assume that distance on the J scale is a linear function of intensity of preference or, alternatively, that the midpoint between two stimuli on the J scale is the point of equality of preference for either. Next we simply observe which I scales are manifest by our respondents. The presence of certain I scales and the absence of others identifies the location of the midpoints between stimuli and consequently the relative distances between pairs of stimuli. This may be illustrated with Figures 4 and 5.

Figure 4 is the four-item J scale, ABCD, onto which we have superimposed the midpoints between each pair of stimuli (denoted by the

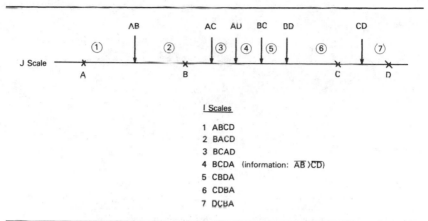

Figure 4: A Four-Stimuli Quantitative J Scale and Its Associated I Scales

arrows). These six midpoints cut the J scale into seven sections, each one associated with a particular preference ranking. These I scales are listed beneath the J scale.

As noted in Figure 4, if these seven I scales are observed, we can deduce that the distance between A and B is greater than the distance between C and D. How? The key is the fourth I scale, BCDA. If observed, it indicates that the midpoint AD is to the left of the midpoint BC. Since B and C are by definition equidistant from the midpoint of the line connecting them, the fact that the midpoint AD is to the left of the BC midpoint indicates that A is farther from B than D is from C. If the segments $\overline{AB}$ and $\overline{CD}$ were equal, the midpoints BC and AD would fall at the same point on the J scale. If, however, $\overline{CD}$ is greater than $\overline{AB}$, the midpoint AD will fall to the right of the BC midpoint as it does in Figure 5.[25] In this case, however, the fourth I scale is CBAD rather than BCDA. All other I scales in Figures 4 and 5 are identical. Thus, in a four-item J scale the middle I scale provides information on the relative distances between the two extreme pairs of stimuli. In empirical situations, however, things are never so straightforward. Often both middle I scales, BCDA and CBAD, will be observed. Distances are usually inferred from the relative frequency of these two preference orderings.

Goodness-of-Fit Criteria

A major problem with unidimensional unfolding theory as we have presented it here is the lack of specific goodness-of-fit criteria such as the

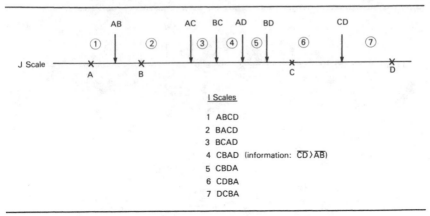

Figure 5: A Second Four-Stimuli Quantitative J Scale and Its I Scales

coefficients of reproducibility and scalability associated with Guttman scaling or the reliability estimates appropriate to summative scales. As a deterministic model, any I scale that does not fit the J scale is sufficient evidence to permit rejection of the hypothesis of unidimensional structure in a set of individual preference rankings. This is, of course, a problem for all deterministic models, such as Guttman scaling. What is required is recognition of the pervasiveness of measurement errors and some set of guidelines to judge the extent of these errors and their consequences on the model. Unfortunately, we have only a rudimentary understanding of the prevalence of error in preference data and its influence on the identification of a common qualitative and quantitative J scale.

General suggestions for evaluating the quality of J scales have been offered. Most obvious perhaps is that the common J scale be dominant, that is, it should be compatible with a greater number of I scales than any other possible J scale. Niemi (1969) points out that given n alternatives, the *minimum* proportion of I scales that must satisfy a common (qualitative) J scale is $2^{n-1}/n!$ Thus, for three stimuli we know that at least two-thirds of the I scales must fit a common J scale. The value of this criterion as a lower bound, however, seems to diminish rapidly. For n = 4, one-third of all individual preference orderings will fit a J scale. For n = 6, only about 4% need fit a common scale.

Several standards have been suggested for ordered-metric J scales. According to Goldberg and Coombs (1963), the fit of 50% + 1 of the set of I scales to a common quantitative J scale is a passable criterion for unidimensionality. Lord and Wilkin (1974: 54-55), however, argue that any such criterion must take into account the number of stimuli in the scale.

Based on simulations, they suggest that 50% is an acceptable criterion for five stimuli and 30% is adequate for six stimuli. With a large number of stimuli, measurement error may preclude identification of a dominant quantitative J scale. But, in the presence of error-laden data, the fit of only a small number of I scales to a J scale may be enough to infer the existence of preferences constrained by a common unidimensional structure. Alternatively, if only a limited number of I scales are consistent with any single J scale, a multidimensional preference structure may underlie individual responses.

The above discussion has hinted at a conclusion that can now be stated explicitly. The assumptions underlying the deterministic unidimensional unfolding model are sufficiently stringent that it is quite rare to find actual data that meet them. When preference data do meet the assumptions, then, as we have seen, the technique allows the researcher to represent respondents and stimuli *jointly* in a unidimensional space in such a way that the relative distances between the points reflect the psychological proximity of the stimuli to the individual's ideal point. The different preference orderings of individuals can be represented on a common scale.

But what conclusions can be drawn if the more typical situation exists— a situation in which one or more of the assumptions underlying the model are violated thereby preventing the I scales from being fitted on a single J scale? Does the analysis provide any useful information in this situation? Fortunately, the unfolding model, as we will see below, allows the researcher to draw some useful conclusions even when analyzing an "imperfectly" ordered set of preference data.

An Example—Measuring Cosmopolitanism

As an example of the use of the unidimensional unfolding model to analyze preferential choice data, we discuss some of the results presented in M. Kent Jennings's (1967) article, "Pre-Adult Orientations to Multiple Levels of Government." In his article Jennings is concerned with the differential interest that high school seniors have in various levels of government—international, national, state, and local—and the extent to which variation in the perceived salience of these political spheres is related to a variety of other political orientations (e.g., knowledge, discourse, and politicization).

Through a series of questions, Jennings is able to ascertain his respondents' rankings of their interest in each of these four political units. Twenty-four possible I scales can be represented by four stimuli, but as we have seen, only seven of these preference orderings can be unfolded to form a single J scale. Based on prior research and theorizing, Jennings

TABLE 16
A Unidimensional Unfolding Scale of Multiple Levels of Government

Scale No.	I Scale	% Fitting I Scale
1	INSL	20.6
2	NISL	14.6
3	NSIL	5.1
4	NSLI - SNIL	4.2 - 1.8
5	SNLI	1.4
6	SLNI	1.8
7	LSNI	3.4
		52.9%
		(N = 1,837)

SOURCE: Adapted from Jennings, 1967: 297.
I = International Affairs, N = National Affairs, S = State Affairs, L = Local Affairs.

expects the seven relevant I scales to be those presented in Table 16. These I scales conform to a basic geopolitical or cosmopolitan ordering with the international-national-state-local order (INSL) and its converse (LSNI) representing the polar types. The interior scales are constructed so that they meet the two other fundamental requirements presumed by the unfolding model—that the I scales end in either the first or last stimulus and that movement from adjacent scales involves the reversal of an adjacent pair of stimuli.

Jennings finds that the I scales of 53% of his respondents can be represented on this common J scale. That is, slightly more than a majority of these high school seniors have a preference ordering represented in Table 16. Respondents having nonscalable preference orderings were assigned the scale type that most closely approximated their I scale. For example, those individuals with I scales INLS and NILS were assigned to the original I scale NISL.[26] Similarly, I scales LSIN and SLIN were assigned to the scale type SLNI. By following this procedure, Jennings is able to assign scale types to nonscalar patterns that involve the least violation of the derived unidimensional solution.

Having assigned the high school seniors to their appropriate scalar type, he then relates their rankings on this cosmopolitanism scale to a variety of cognitive, behavioral, and affective orientations. Not surprisingly, he finds that students who are more cosmopolitan in orientation are more knowledgeable about and interested in world affairs, more tolerant of social and political diversity, and more trustful of higher level governmental systems.

Jennings's article demonstrates four important points about applications of the unfolding method. First, as we have pointed out earlier, it is indeed rare to find preferential choice data that only vary along a single underlying continuum. Jennings's results are not atypical—the discovery of a dominant J scale that can accommodate a significant proportion of the I scales, but with some preference orderings that cannot be represented in the unidimensional space. Substantively, this evidence indicates that not all of the subjects are viewing the stimuli from the same perspective. Instead, it is obvious, as Jennings observes, that "a number of variables other than the geopolitical space encompassed may reasonably impinge upon the differential saliency of the four system levels" (Jennings, 1967: 299). Second, Jennings's analysis shows that the model is not rendered useless in the face of a set of less than perfectly ordered data. On the contrary, the requirements imposed by the model can be used as a guide to assign scale types to the nonscalar patterns. Third, this example illustrates again the importance of theoretical guidance of research questions.[27] Jennings chose to investigate a particular J scale that met his expectations concerning the salience of levels of government. A substantial number of his students fit the cosmopolitanism scale, and it demonstrated predictive validity when correlated with other political variables. This does not mean Jennings necessarily reported the "best" scale that might be constructed from his data. A considerably greater number of students fit two other J scales: 66% fit an NLIS J scale while 65% fit an LNIS scale. Yet neither J scale has the intuitive interpretation of the cosmopolitan scale that Jennings reported. Finally, we have seen that since the unfolding method is used to scale people as well as stimuli, the derived scale scores can be related to other measures of interest.

Trust in Government: A Second Example

In 1976, the Center for Political Studies at the University of Michigan, as part of their election year national survey, asked respondents to rank their trust in the various institutions of our national government—the President (P), the Congress (C), and the Supreme Court (S).[28] In Table 17 we present the possible I scales and the frequency with which the survey respondents ascribed to each.

What J scale might underlie the preferences of the respondents? With three stimuli, three J scales are possible. Each has a legitimate interpretation in light of the reference to institutional trust. The scale CSP/PSC suggests trust may be perceived to be a function of size of organization. Alternatively, trust may be a function of the possibility of electoral accountability. In this case we might observe scale PCS/SCP. Finally,

TABLE 17
Trust in Government, 1976

CSP	245	
CPS	265	
SCP	380	
SPC	354	
PCS	263	
PSC	232	

N = 1,739

All Possible J Scales

Size (CSP)	Electoral Accountability (PCS)	Representativeness/Support for Equal Rights (CPS/SPC)
CSP	PCS	CPS
SCP	CPS	PCS
SPC	CSP	PSC
PSC	SCP	SPC
1,211/1,739	1,153/1,739	1,114/1,739
70%	66%	64%

trust could be a function of past performance or accessibility. The dominance of J scale CPS/SPC might indicate the growth of diffuse support with the preservation of minority of majority rights by each institution. Lacking sufficient cause to prefer one hypothesis over another, we submit all three to the data.

The bottom half of Table 17 describes each of the J scales and the proportion of the sample that fits each. For three stimuli, there must exist a common J scale that fits at least two-thirds of the respondents (see above). While no J scale performs much better than the others, only one, the CSP/PSC scale, fits a greater than minimum proportion of the sample; that is, 70% of the respondents fit this J scale. Acceptance of the hypothesis that trust is a function of the size of government institutions requires corroborating evidence, but is suggested by our unfolding analysis.

Conclusion

The purpose of this chapter has been to provide an introduction to the unfolding model in a single dimension, paying particular attention to the logic underlying this scaling method. The unidimensional unfolding model attempts to scale both stimuli and individuals so that the preference orderings among various individuals is consistent with the placement of those individuals on a common continuum. The psychological proximity of the stimuli to the individuals, as revealed by the ranking of their preferences, is reflected in the relative distances between the points in the unidimensional space.

What does it mean if a set of I scales can be unfolded along a single dimension? Logically, this implies that a particular stimulus is closer on the J scale to a given individual than is another stimulus if and only if it is more proximal psychologically. This property allows the researcher to represent the various preference orderings in a unidimensional space. Substantively, a perfect unfolding scale suggests that "the preferences were generated by people having different ideals but viewing the stimuli in a similar manner" (Dawes, 1972: 67). In other words, they evaluate the stimuli differently (as revealed by their different preference orderings), but their differences are constrained in such a way that they lie along the same dimension (as revealed by the existence of a common J scale). Voters, for example, may evaluate candidates differently depending on the political ideologies they represent, but as long as ideology is the sole criterion used in their judgmental process, then their preferences can be represented in a unidimensional space.

Conversely, if a set of I scales *cannot* be unfolded in a common dimension, not only do their preferences differ but they also do not share a common frame of reference for their preferences. In other words, they are not viewing the stimuli along the same dimension. Instead, they are focusing on different attributes of the phenomena in question. To refer to our earlier example, voters may be reacting to the candidates not only on the basis of a common political ideology but also in terms of perceived personal attributes and professional qualifications.

As we pointed out at the beginning of this chapter, unidimensional unfolding has been infrequently used in the social sciences. This is not to say it has been proved useless in empirical research. As we have illustrated in this chapter, unfolding has been put to important use by political scientists. Niemi (1969) provides an important link between this empirically based model of preferential choice and theories of voting. Weisberg (1972) and Karns (1972) have examined congressional voting behavior using a "proximity" model, a relative of the unfolding model developed for use with dichotomous choice data.[29]

Unfolding has also been used by psychologists, sociologists, and economists. Coombs (1950, 1964) demonstrates the applicability of unfolding theory to the study of gambling and the prediction of grade expectations. Goldberg and Coombs (1962) analyze the childbearing of Detroit women with respect to their preferences for an ideal family size. Unfolding has proved useful in advertising and marketing research (Taylor, 1969). Runkel (1956) displays the relevance of this method for communication research. Israel (1959) analyzes intragroup pressure from the perspective of unfolding theory.

Beyond these examples, however, unfolding is rarely found in the social science literatures. Collection of data may be one problem. Rating or pick methods are much simpler collection procedures than the ranking methods required by the unfolding model. Perhaps the failure of researchers to find dominant J scales when rank-order data are collected is one reason for lack of examples in the literature. The lack of a goodness-of-fit measure is also troublesome. Ability to estimate scale reliabilities, an attractive feature of the summative scaling, is underdeveloped for unfolding analysis. Finally, the methodology gets very unwieldy beyond five stimuli. The lack of widely available computer software to assist analyses of order data may present some barriers to use of the model. We hope these problems will be alleviated as the methodology becomes more widely recognized.

7. CONCLUSION

This monograph has discussed several methods for scaling empirical data. In scaling, the researcher analyzes a set of items with the initial purpose of discovering whether they represent a dimension that is itself neither directly observable nor measurable. If the items as a group satisfy specific criteria for a scale, the researcher infers the existence of the latent dimension. Among the many questions that may be asked about the dimension is whether it is shared by various subgroups in the population, the various causal mechanisms that give rise to the particular dimension, and the extent to which it is related to a variety of psychological and behavioral phenomena.

The term *dimension* has been used in the singular in the above paragraph because all of the scaling models considered in this monograph are intended to place items and/or subjects on a single, common continuum. While multidimensional techniques have gained a great deal of attention in recent years, for reasons outlined in Chapter 1, we believe unidimensional scaling models will continue to play a prominent role in the social sciences. Most important, unidimensional models coincide with the use of unidimensional language in social science theories—language that is intended to clarify the meaning of those theories.

These models, then, are alike in that they all attempt to represent data in a unidimensional space. However, they differ from one another in a

TABLE 18
A Comparison of Scaling Models

	Likert	Guttman	Coombs
1. Definition of unidimensionality:	equal and high correlations among all items; accounts for all systematic variance among items	perfect reproducibility of item responses from scale scores	consistency of all preference rankings with a common J scale
2. Interpretation of scale scores:	"average" position	cumulativeness or extremeness	ideal preference (range of preference can be determined in some data collection schemes)
3. Respondents located on dimension?: Items located on dimension?:	yes no	yes yes	yes yes
4a. Location of items at the same point point on the dimension:		same extremeness of stimuli	same perception of items
4b. Location of respondents at the same point on the dimension:	same "average" position	same acceptance of extremes	same ideal points and preference ordering
5. Opposite ends of the continuum:	respondents with most different average preferences	respondents with the least and the most extreme preferences	respondents with opposite preference rankings of all stimuli
6. Trace line patterns:	monotonically increasing or decreasing	step function	single peaked (i.e., changes direction at most once from up to down)
7. Kind of data:	single stimulus	single stimulus	preferential choice
8. Level of measurement scale:	interval	ordinal	ordinal or ordered metric (approximately interval for more than 5 stimuli)

number of specific ways including having varying conceptions of dimensionality. Table 18 presents some of the distinguishing features of summative, cumulative, and unfolding scaling. While the table is largely self-explanatory, we would like to emphasize the differences in the interpretation of scales that are constructed according to each of these scaling methods. These differences in interpretation, in turn, reflect the distinct meaning of dimensionality as conceived by Likert, Guttman, and Coombs in developing these models.

Both Likert and Guttman scales are scored simply by summing the number of positive responses to the set of items. But the totals do not reveal the same property about positions of the respondents on the dimensions. Individuals who fit a Guttman scale are indicating a willingness to accept anything up to a certain extreme (for them) position. Niemi and Weisberg (1974) note that this property of Guttman scaling is often misinterpreted. All too often, those who apply Guttman procedures mistakenly interpret their results as indicating their respondents' preferred positions on the particular dimension. In other words, Guttman scales do not imply single-peaked preference orderings. An individual with a scale score of 4 could have a preferred or ideal position anywhere from 0 to 4. Likert respondents, on the other hand, are denoting their *average* or most likely position on the dimension.

In its conception of respondent location, Likert scaling is somewhat similar to unfolding in the sense that a respondent is providing some information about his or her "best" position on the underlying continuum. But we get more information from preferential choice data if a common J scale exists for in this situation respondents provide an interlocking ranking describing preferences for positions for the entire continuum in addition to an ideal position. Thus, only unfolding scales imply the existence of single-peaked preference orderings. Furthermore, unfolding (as does Guttman scaling) permits the researcher to position stimuli on a common dimension with respondents. This is not the purpose of Likert scaling.

There also exists a fundamental distinction in the interpretation of cumulative scales and unfolding scales. As we have pointed out, the former is a measure of limitations or maximums; the latter is a measure of proximity or nearness to an ideal position.

In summary, Guttman scale scores reveal the acceptance of a specific degree of extremeness in position, Likert scores indicate average position, and unfolding scores imply preference orderings with an ideal position on the underlying continuum. Each of these interpretations is based on a distinct conception of dimensionality.

Finally, we would like to emphasize the importance of theory and external evidence in applications of scaling. Scaling should not take place in a theoretical vacuum. Usually researchers are investigating a general hypothesis—implicitly if not explicitly—that individuals are responding to a set of items on the basis of a shared perception of their content. Choice of a scaling model will thus depend not only on the type of data available for analysis and the intended use of the results of the analysis but also on the substantive nature of the hypothesis under investigation.

Ideally, theory-guided applications of scaling will utilize external as well as internal sources of evidence to validate specific interpretations of data. In other words, the internal criteria outlined with regard to each of the scaling models discussed in this monograph need to be supplemented by externally derived evidence (Carmines and Zeller, 1974; Zeller and Carmines, 1976, 1980; Berry, 1980). Stated alternatively, the particular application of scaling needs to be placed in an explicit theoretical context.

This requirement, moreover, is equally relevant to applications of multidimensional scaling methods. Indeed, unidimensional and multidimensional scaling models can complement one another in this regard. Multidimensional analyses may be useful in confirming the unidimensional structure underlying data; unidimensional methods may facilitate interpretation of multidimensional configurations. And regardless of the type of analyses performed, theory plays an indispensable role in understanding results and guiding research.

NOTES

1. While scaling has often been associated with the measurement of attitudes, values, and opinions, it need not be conceived of in such a restrictive manner. Instead, scaling and scale construction are of central concern in the measurement of any phenomena—objective conditions as well as subjective states.

2. Other components of data may be relevant to the relationship among stimuli, responses, and persons. For example, data located at any point in this three-dimensional scheme may not be immutable, that is, time might influence interrelationships in the matrix. In the interest of parsimony, we will ignore such factors.

3. If we know the real weights of these objects, we could also use these data for scaling persons by ranking each individual on his accuracy of perceptions. Thus the same data can serve multiple purposes.

4. Actually, Thurstone discussed five distinct cases of the Law of Comparative Judgment. Our discussion is intended only to convey the general ideas underlying the law rather than consider the specific differences among the cases. The method of equal appearing intervals, which we discuss below, is based on the Law of Categorical Judgment, a special case of Thurstone's general judgment model. The Law of Categorical Judgment focuses on judgments that require the respondent to place the stimuli into a number of ordered categories instead of simply evaluating a pair of stimuli.

5. The basic limitation of the method of paired comparisons is the limited number of items that can be scaled. For example, if comparative judgments are to be made on each pair of stimuli, then each individual must make $n(n-1)/2$ comparative judgments where n is the number of stimuli: 20 stimuli will require 190 comparative judgments, 30 stimuli will require 455 judgments, and 40 will require 780 judgments. The method of successive intervals is a slightly less restrictive scaling model than the equal-appearing method in that it does not require that the widths of the intervals be equal. This allows the scale values obtained from this method to be linearly related to those obtained from the method of paired comparisons over the *complete range* rather than only for the nonextreme values as in the method of equal-appearing intervals. For a detailed discussion of all three Thurstone scaling methods, see Edwards (1957).

6. Nunnally (1978: 79) has pointed out a further problem with Thurstone scales: the difficulty of finding statements with the appropriate nonmonotonic probability trace lines

that will fit the model. As he observes, "attitude statements tend to fit this model only if they are 'double-barreled'—only if they say two things, of which one is good and the other bad." But we have already noted that such ambiguous statements are generally to be avoided in the construction of any scale.

7. Likert did not provide an explicit mathematical model for this scaling procedure. This section is based on the writings of psychometricians that followed Likert who attempted to place his work within the general study of test theories (see Green, 1954; Nunnally, 1978; Torgerson, 1958; Schuessler, 1971).

8. In one sense, Cronbach's alpha is a generalization of the Spearman-Brown prophecy formula. Novick and Lewis (1967) have demonstrated that coefficient alpha for a test having 2N items is equal to the average value of the alpha coefficients obtained for all possible combinations of items into two half-tests. (For a scale composed of 2N items, there are $(2N)! / [2(N!) (N!)]$ possible split halves.)

9. This section focuses on correlational methods rather than t tests because they are now easily accessible and, as noted earlier, retain more information than the criterion of internal consistency or t-test procedure. The logic of correcting the relationship between the total scale and the individual item discussed here applies to the criterion of internal consistency as well.

10. Also see Curetin (1966) and Lord and Novick (1968).

11. Except in the special case of subsets of one item.

12. For a general introduction to factor analysis, see the Kim and Mueller (1978a, 1978b) volumes in this series. The role of factor analysis in assessing the reliability and validity of multiple-item scales is treated in greater detail in Carmines and Zeller (1979) and Zeller and Carmines (1980).

13. Jöreskog (1971) proposes a statistical test for assessing whether a set of items is due to a single factor. Our own experience indicates that it is quite rare to find scale items that are unidimensional according to this test.

14. Nunnally (1978: 73) argues that despite the intuitive appeal of Guttman's scaling model, its deterministic assumption is unrealistic. It is unlikely for most items to have Guttman-type trace lines as depicted in Figure 1.

15. In the large sample case, the most available computer program—SPSS-Guttman Scale—is based on the Goodenough-Edwards technique.

16. The modal response category for any item is the category that contains the largest proportion of responses. If, for example, an item contains 40% favorable responses and 60% unfavorable, the proportion of responses in the item's modal category is .60.

17. A PRE statistic is defined as follows:

PRE = (error by rule 2 − error by rule 1) / error by rule 2.

18. In contrast to each of these coefficients, Pearson's product-moment coefficient (or its equivalent, phi, for the 2×2 table) will not equal 1.0 if any cases fall in the off-diagonal cells.

19. We do not consider expected CR extensively because it is computationally unwieldy. A computer program for assessing chance reproductibility from item marginals is available from the authors on request.

20. The unfolding model can also be used to analyze data collected by the paired comparison technique. This data collection method involves presenting a set of stimuli to respondents two at a time and asking them to select the one they prefer. A rank ordering can be derived for each respondent by presenting various combinations of the paired stimuli.

21. The combinatorial $\binom{n}{2}$ is equal to $n! / [2!(n-2)!]$. Kirkpatrick (1974) indicates that this number is also equivalent to $(n^2 - n) / 2$.

22. n stimuli may be ordered n! ways. However, half of these orderings are mirror images of one another and hence equivalent as J scales. Thus, the number of possible J scales of n stimuli is $n!/2$.

23. The combinatorial $\binom{n}{x}$ refers to the number of possible subsets of size x taken from a set of size n. $\binom{n}{x}$ is equivalent to $(n!)/[x!(n-x)!]$. For example, the number of subsets of 4 from 6 items is $(6!)/[4!(6-4)!] = 15$.

24. McClelland and Coombs (1975) provide a general algorithm, ORDMET, for computing metric distances from information about the relative sizes of line segments. The inference of metric distances in simple cases is described by Coombs (1964) and Long and Wilkins (1974).

25. The relative lengths of line segments of the J scale can be computed given the relative location of the stimuli and the midpoint orderings. All that is required is knowledge of the rules for manipulating mathematical inequalities. For a four-stimuli scale, if the midpoint of AD precedes BC, then we know that $(A+D)/2 < (B+C)/2$. This implies that $(A+D) < (B+C)$, an inequality that may be transformed into $(D-C) < (B-A)$. This result is simply that the length of segment $\overline{CD}$ is less than the distance from A to B, $\overline{AB}$. If the midpoint BC precedes AD, then $(A+D)/2 > (B+C)/2$ which implies that $(D-C) > (B-A)$ or $\overline{CD} > \overline{AB}$. Assign numbers to the stimuli of Figure 4 and prove this to yourself.

26. For his justification for this procedure, see Jennings (1967: 299-301). Nonscalable rank orders were not assigned to the INSL or LSNI I scales.

27. Without some guidance as to the possible underlying continuum, trial-and-error experimentation can become unwieldy very quickly as the number of stimuli increase. There are $n!/2$ possible qualitative J scales for a set of n stimuli and many quantitative J scales associated with each. For four stimuli, 24 possible ordered-metric J scales exist: $(4!/2) \times 2$. Over 100,000 $[(6!/2) \times 286]$ quantitative J scales are possible with six stimuli (Long and Wilken, 1974).

28. Trust in political parties was also asked. Preliminary analysis suggested there was little differentiation of parties by respondents—political parties were uniformly the least trusted institution.

29. Respondents are asked to accept or reject each of n stimuli. Data collected this way are referred to as a "pick" method as opposed to an "order" method and are identical to data collected for Guttman scaling. The pattern supporting the hypothesis of one dimension underlying individual "pick" strategies, however, is not the triangle expected by Guttman, but a parallelogram. Weisberg (1972) discusses the proximity model in detail. Coombs (1964) discusses the analogous parallelogram model for incomplete ranking data.

REFERENCES

ABRAMSON, P. R. and A. W. FINIFTER (1981) "On the meaning of political trust: New evidence from items introduced in 1978." American Journal of Political Science 25: 297-307.

ADORNO, T. W., E. FRENKEL-BRUNSWIK, D. J. LEVINSON, and R. N. SANFORD (1950) The Authoritarian Personality. New York: W. W. Norton.

ALEXANDER, C. N. and J. PERRY (1967) "A new technique for improving cumulative scales." Public Opinion Quarterly 31: 110-115.

ALLARDT, E., P. JARTTI, F. JYRKILA, and Y. LITTUNEN (1959) "On the cumulative nature of leisure activities." Acta Sociologica 3: 165-172.

ALWIN, D. F. (1973) "The use of factor analysis in the construction of linear composites in social research." Sociological Methods and Research 2: 191-214.

ANDERSON, L. F., M. W. WATTS, Jr., and A. R. WILCOX (1966) Legislative Roll-Call Analysis. Evanston, IL: Northwestern University Press.

ARNOLD, W. R. (1965) "Continuities in research-scaling delinquent behavior." Social Problems 13: 59-66.

BENNETT, J. F. and W. L. HAYS (1960) "Multidimensional unfolding: Determining the dimensionality of ranked preference data." Psychometrika 25: 27-43.

BERRY, W. (1979) "On the use of external criteria to interpret spatial structures: A note of caution but encouragement." Political Methodology 6: 425-436.

BLALOCK, H. M. (1970) "Estimating measurement error using multiple indicators and several points in time." American Sociological Review 35: 101-111.

CARMINES, E. G. and R. A. ZELLER (1980) Reliability and Validity Assessment. Sage University Paper series on Quantitative Applications in the Social Sciences, 07-017. Beverly Hills, CA: Sage.

CARMINES, E. G. and R. A. ZELLER (1974) "On establishing the empirical dimensionality of theoretical terms: An analytical example." Political Methodology 1: 75-96.

CARNEIRO, R. (1962) "Scale analysis as an instrument for the study of cultural evolution." Southwestern Journal of Anthropology 18: 149-169.

CHILTON, R. J. (1969) "A review and comparison of simple statistical tests for scalogram analysis." American Sociological Review 38: 238-245.

CHILTON, R. J. (1966) "Computer generated data and the statistical significance of scalograms." Sociometry 29: 175-181.

CITRIN, J. (1974) "Comment: The political relevance of trust in government." American Political Science Review 68: 973-988.

CLAUSEN, A. R. (1973) How Congressmen Decide: A Policy Focus. New York: St. Martin's.

CLAUSEN, A. R. and C. E. VAN HORN (1977) "How to analyze too many roll calls and related issues in dimensional analysis." Political Methodology 4: 313-331.

CLOGG, C. C. (1977) "Unrestricted and restricted maximum likelihood latent structure analysis: A manual for users." University Park: The Pennsylvania State University, Population Issues Research Office.

COOMBS, C. H. (1964) A Theory of Data. New York: John Wiley.

COOMBS, C. H. (1950) "Psychological scaling without a unit of measurement." Psychological Review 57: 145-158.

CRONBACH, L. J. (1951) "Coefficient alpha and the internal structure of tests." Psychometrika 16: 294-334.

CURETON, E. E. (1966) "Corrected item-test correlations." Psychometrika 31: 93-96.

DAWES, R. M. (1972) Fundamentals of Attitude Measurement. New York: John Wiley.

DAYTON, C. M. and G. B. MACREADY (1980) "A scaling model with response errors and intrinsically unscalable respondents." Psychometrika 45: 343-356.

EDWARDS, A. (1957) Techniques of Attitude Scale Construction. Englewood Cliffs, NJ: Prentice-Hall.

EDWARDS, A. (1948) "On guttman's scale analysis." Educational and Psychological Measurement 8: 313-318.

FESTINGER, L. (1947) "The treatment of qualitative data by scale analysis." Psychological Bulletin 44: 149-161.

GOLDBERG, D. and C. H. COOMBS (1962) "Some applications of unfolding theory to fertility analysis," pp. 311-332 in G. M. Maranell (ed.) Scaling: A Sourcebook for Behavioral Scientists. Chicago: Aldine

GOODENOUGH, W. H. (1963) "Some applications of guttman scale analysis to ethnography and culture theory." Southwestern Journal of Anthropology 19: 235-250.

93

GOODENOUGH, W. H. (1944) "A technique for scale analysis." Educational and Psychological Measurement 4: 179-190.

GOODMAN, L. A. (1975) "A new model for scaling response patterns: An application of the quasi-independence concept." Journal of the American Statistical Association 70: 755-768.

GORDEN, R. L. (1977) Unidimensional Scaling of Social Variables: Concepts and Procedures. New York: Free Press.

GREEN, B. F. (1956) "A method of scalogram analysis using summary statistics." Psychometrika 21: 79-88.

GREEN, B. F. (1954) "Attitude measurement," pp. 335-369 in G. Lindzey (ed.) Handbook of Social Psychology. Reading, MA: Addison-Wesley.

GREEN, P. E. and F. J. CARMONE (1969) "Multidimensional unfolding: An introduction and comparison of nonmetric unfolding techniques." Journal of Marketing Research 6: 330-341.

GREENE, V. L. and E. G. CARMINES (1979) "Assessing the reliability of linear composites," pp. 160-175 in K. F. Schuessler (ed.) Sociological Methodology 1980. San Francisco: Jossey-Bass.

GUTTMAN, L. L. (1950) "The basis for scalogram analysis," pp. 60-90 in S. A. Stouffer et al. (eds.) Measurement and Prediction. Princeton, NJ: Princeton University Press.

GUTTMAN, L. L. (1947) "On Festinger's evaluation of scale analysis." Psychological Bulletin 44: 451-465.

GUTTMAN, L. L. (1944) "A basis for scaling qualitative data." American Sociological Review 9: 139-150.

HAYS, W. L. and J. F. BENNETT (1961) "Multidimensional unfolding: Determining configuration from complete rank order preference data. Psychometrika 26: 221-238.

ISRAEL, J. (1959) "Measurement of cross-pressures in groups by the unfolding technique." Acta Sociologica 4: 1-7.

JENNINGS, M. K. (1967) "Pre-adult orientations to multiple levels of government." Midwest Journal of Political Science 11: 291-317.

JENNINGS, M. K. and R. G. NIEMI (1981) Generations and Politics. Princeton, NJ: Princeton, NJ: Princeton University Press.

JENNINGS, M. K. and R. G. NIEMI (1974) The Political Character of Adolescence: The Influence of Families and Schools. Princeton, NJ: Princeton University Press.

JORESKOG, K. G. (1971) "Statistical analysis of sets of congeneric tests." Psychometrika 36: 109-133.

KARNS, D. A. (1972) "Legislative context and roll call analysis: Foreign policy voting behavior in the senate." Unpublished manuscript, Cornell University.

KIM, J. and C. W. MUELLER (1978a) Introduction to Factor Analysis: What It Is and How To Do It. Beverly Hills, CA: Sage.

KIM, J. and C. W. MUELLER (1978b) Factor Analysis: Statistical Methods and Practical Issues. Beverly Hills, CA: Sage.

KIM, J. and J. RABJOHN (1980) "Binary variables and index construction," pp. 120-159 in K. Schuessler (ed.) Sociological Methodology 1980. San Francisco: Jossey-Bass.

KIRKPATRICK, S. A. (1974) Quantitative Analysis of Political Data. Columbus, OH: Charles E. Merrill.

KRUSKAL, J. B. and M. WISH (1978) Multidimensional Scaling. Beverly Hills, CA: Sage.

LAZARSFELD, P. F. (1950) "The logical and mathematical foundation of latent structure analysis," pp. 454-472 in S. A. Stouffer et al. (eds.) Measurement and Prediction. Princeton, NJ: Princeton University Press.

LAZARSFELD, P. F. and N. W. HENRY (1968) Latent Structure Analysis. Boston: Houghton-Mifflin.

94

LIKERT, R. (1974) "A method of constructing an attitude scale," pp. 233-243 in G. M. Maranell (ed.) Scaling: A Sourcebook for Behavioral Scientists. Chicago: Aldine.

LIKERT, R. (1931) "A technique for the measurement of attitudes." Archives of Psychology. New York: Columbia University Press.

LONG, J. F. and P. H. WILKEN (1974) "A fully nonmetric unfolding technique: Interval values from ordinal data," pp. 11-60 in H. M. Blalock (ed.) Measurement in the Social Sciences. Chicago: Aldine.

LORD, F. M. and M. R. NOVICK (1968) Statistical Theories of Mental Test Scores. Reading, MA: Addison-Wesley.

MacRAE, D., Jr. (1970) Issues and Parties in Legislative Voting: Methods of Statistical Analysis. New York: Harper & Row.

MANIS, J. G., M. J. BRAWER, C. L. HUNT, and L. C. KERCHER (1963) "Validating a mental health scale." American Sociological Review 28: 108-116.

MARANELL, G. M. [ed.] (1974) Scaling: A Sourcebook for Behavioral Scientists. Chicago: Aldine.

McCLELLAND, G. and C. H. COOMBS (1975) "ORDMET: A general algorithm for constructing all numerical solutions to ordered metric data." Psychometrika 40: 269-290.

MENZEL, H. (1953) "A new coefficient for scalogram analysis." Public Opinion Quarterly 17: 268-280.

MILBRATH, L. W. (1965) Political Participation: How and Why Do People Get Involved in Politics? Skokie, IL: Rand McNally.

MILLER, A. H. (1974a) "Political issues and trust in government: 1964-1970." American Political Science Review 68: 951-972.

MILLER, A. H. (1974b) "Rejoinder to 'comment' by Jack Citrin: Political discontent or ritualism." American Political Science Review 68: 989-1001.

MILLER, D. C. (1970) Handbook of Research Design and Social Measurement. New York: David McKay.

MOKKEN, R. J. (1971) A Theory and Procedure of Scale Analysis. The Hague: Mouton.

MOSES, L., et al. (1967) "Scaling data on inter-nation action." Science 156: 1054-1059.

MURPHY, G. and R. LIKERT (1937) Public Opinion and the Individual. New York: Harper & Row.

NESVOLD, B. A. (1971) "Scalogram analysis of political violence," in J. V. Gillespie and B. A. Nesvold (eds.) Macro-Quantitative Analysis. Beverly Hills, CA: Sage.

NIE, N. H., C. H. HULL, J. G. JENKINS, K. STEINBRENNER, and D. H. BENT (1975) SPSS: Statistical Package for the Social Sciences. New York: McGraw-Hill.

NIEMI, R. G. (1969) "Majority decision making with partial unidimensionality." American Political Science Review 63: 488-497.

NIEMI, R. G. and H. F. WEISBERG (1974) "Single-peakedness and Guttman scales: Concept and measurement." Public Choice 20: 33-45.

NOVICK, M. R. and C. LEWIS (1967) "Coefficient alpha and the reliability of composite measurements." Psychometrika 32: 1-13.

NUNNALLY, J. C. (1978) Psychometric Theory. New York: McGraw-Hill.

NYE, F. I. and J. F. SHORT Jr. (1957) "Scaling delinquent behavior." American Sociological Review 22: 326-331.

PETERS, C. C. and W. R. VAN VOORBIS (1940) Statistical Procedures and Their Mathematical Bases. New York: McGraw-Hill.

PODELL, L. and J. C. PERKINS (1957) "A Guttman scale for sexual experience—a methodological note." Journal of Abnormal and Social Psychology 54: 420-422.

RIESELBACH, L. N. (1966) The Roots of Isolationism: Congressional Voting and Presidential Leadership in Foreign Policy. Indianapolis: Bobbs-Merrill.

ROBINSON, J. P. (1973) "Toward a more appropriate use of Guttman scaling." Public Opinion Quarterly 37: 260-267.

ROBINSON, J. P., R. ATHANASIOU, and K. HEAD (1969) Measures of Occupational Attitudes and Occupational Characteristics. Ann Arbor: University of Michigan, Institute for Social Research.

ROBINSON, J. P., J. G. RUSK, and K. HEAD (1968) Measurement of Political Attitudes. Ann Arbor: University of Michigan, Institute for Social Research.

ROBINSON, J. P. and P. R. SHAVER (1970) Measures of Social Psychological Attitudes. Ann Arbor: University of Michigan, Institute for Social Research.

ROHDE, D. W. and H. J. SPAETH (1976) Supreme Court Decision Making. San Francisco: W. H. Freeman.

ROSENBERG, M. (1965) Society and the Adolescent Self-Image. Princeton, NJ: Princeton University Press.

RUNKEL, P. J. (1956) "Cognitive similarity in facilitating communication." Sociometry 19: 178-191.

RUNKEL, P. J. and J. E. McGRATH (1972) Research on Human Behavior: A Systematic Guide to Method. New York: Holt, Rinehart and Winston.

SAGI, P. C. (1959) "A statistical test for the significance of a coefficient of reproducibility." Psychometrika 24: 19-27.

SCHOOLER, C. (1968) "A note of extreme caution on the use of Guttman scales." American Journal of Sociology 74: 296-301.

SCHUBERT, G. (1965) The Judicial Mind: Attitude and Ideologies of Supreme Court Justices, 1946-1963. Evanston, IL: Northwestern University Press.

SCHUESSLER, K. F. (1971) Analyzing Social Data: A Statistical Orientation. Boston, MA: Houghton-Mifflin.

SCHUESSLER, K. F. (1961) "A note on statistical significance of scalogram." Sociometry 24. 312 318.

SCHUESSLER, K. F. (1952) "Item selection in scale analysis." American Sociological Review 17: 183-192.

SCHWARTZ, R. D. and J. C. MILLER (1964) "Legal evolution and societal complexity." American Journal of Sociology 70: 159-169.

SCOTT, W. A. (1968) "Attitude measurement," pp. 204-273 in G. Lindzey and E. Aronson (eds.) The Handbook of Social Psychology. Reading, MA: Addison-Wesley.

SEWELL, W. H. (1941) "The development of a sociometric scale." Sociometry 3: 279-297.

SHIVELY, W. P. (1980) The Craft of Political Research: A Primer. Englewood Cliffs, NJ: Prentice-Hall.

SNOW, P. G. (1966) "A scalogram analysis of political development." American Behavioral Scientist 9: 33-36.

STOUFFER, S. A., E. F. BORGATTA, D. G. HAYS, and A. F. HENRY (1952) "A technique for improving cumulative scales." Public Opinion Quarterly 16: 273-291.

SUCHMAN, E. (1950) "The utility of scalogram analysis," pp. 122-171 in S. A. Stouffer (ed.) Measurement and Prediction. Princeton, NJ: Princeton University Press.

SULLIVAN, J. L. and S. FELDMAN (1979) Multiple Indicators: An Introduction. Beverly Hills, CA: Sage.

TAYLOR, J. R. (1969) "Unfolding theory applied to market-segmentation." Journal of Advertising Research 9: 39-46.

THURSTONE, L. L. (1929) "Fechner's law and the method of equal-appearing intervals." Journal of Experimental Psychology 12: 214-224.

THURSTONE, L. L. (1927) "A law of comparative judgment." Psychological Review 34: 273-286.

THURSTONE, L. L. and E. J. CHAVE (1929) The Measurement of Attitudes. Chicago: University of Chicago Press.

TODD, J. R. (1977) "Toward an operationally interpretable procedure for evaluating Guttman scales." Political Methodology 4: 153-170.

TORGERSON, W. S. (1958) Theory and Methods of Scaling. New York: John Wiley.
UDY, S. Jr. (1958) "'Bureaucratic' elements in organizations: Some research findings." American Sociological Review 73: 415-418.
VERBA, S. and N. H. NIE (1972) Participation in America: Political Democracy and Social Equality. New York: Harper & Row.
WALLIN, P. (1953) "A Guttman scale for measuring women's neighborliness." American Journal of Sociology 59: 243-246.
WEISBERG, H. F. (1974) "Dimensionland: An excursion into spaces." American Journal of Political Science 18: 743-776.
WEISBERG, H. F. (1972) "Scaling models for legislative roll-call analysis." American Political Science Review 66: 1306-1315.
YOUNG, F. W. and R. C. YOUNG (1962) "The sequence and direction of community growth: A cross-cultural generalization." Rural Sociology 27: 374-386.
ZELLER, R. A. and E. G. CARMINES (1980) Measurement in the Social Sciences: The Link Between Theory and Data. New York: Cambridge University Press.
ZELLER, R. A. and E. G. CARMINES (1978) Statistical Analysis of Social Data. Skokie, IL: Rand McNally.
ZELLER, R. A. and E. G. CARMINES (1976) "Factor scaling, external consistency, and the measurement of theoretical constructs." Political Methodology 3: 215-252.

JOHN P. McIVER is Associate Professor of Political Science at the University of Colorado, Boulder. His research interests include American politics, public policy analysis (specifically applied to the delivery of urban services), and statistical methodologies. He has published articles on each of these topics in the American Journal of Political Science, Policy and Politics, *and* Policy Studies Journal *as well as in several edited collections. His current work focuses on the impact of political issues on the acquisition and retention of partisanship.*

EDWARD G. CARMINES is Rudy Professor of Political Science at Indiana University, Bloomington. He received his Ph.D. from the State University of New York at Buffalo. His primary research interests are in American politics and methodology, and he has published articles in these areas in various journals, including the American Political Science Review, Journal of Politics, *and* American Journal of Political Science. *He is the coauthor, with Richard A. Zeller, of* Statistical Analysis of Social Data *and* Measurement in the Social Sciences: The Link Between Theory and Data, *and, with James A. Stimson, of* Issue Evolution. *His current research focuses on the origins, evolution, and resolution of political issues in American politics.*